How Steve Became RALPH

D1120709

Steve Buechler

Praise for *How Steve Became Ralph*

"*How Steve Became Ralph* is an odyssey in every sense of the word. Buechler transforms a devastating cancer diagnosis into a literary quest infused with intelligence, mindfulness, humor, and hope."

—Carolyn Redman, Author of *News From Lake Boobbegone*

"Steve Buechler's *How Steve Became Ralph* is an unusual cancer memoir as it's not about death and dying rather about living and thriving. The book is filled with life lessons injected with ample doses of the author's quirky sense of humor. A compelling read!"

—Simi K. Rao, Physician and Author

"Steve (or now Ralph) reminds us, healthy or ill, that life, with all its challenges, is worth living. It shows us the importance of seeing the glass half full rather than half empty, the necessity of setting real priorities in our lives and that keeping an open mind for all the goodness that our journey can offer, even in trying situations, can be ultimately rewarding to ourselves and others around us. It also underscores that patients have a major role in their healing process, which cannot be merely passive. More importantly, love from our family members and our friends, and even from our health care providers (and ourselves) can achieve the best possible results. Good reading to re-set perspectives and to help appreciate and treasure our lives, one day at a time."

—Gina Cunto-Amesty, Physician

"A thoughtful encouraging expression of one man's odyssey beyond a diagnosis of leukemia. This is a courageous plowing-through months of testing and treatment supported by family, friends and health care providers. Punctuated by personal insights and small quips of humor, Steve Buechler delves into his physical, psycho-social and spiritual processes as he works with the health care community and a cord blood transplant. A good read for a health care provider, patient, or caregiver."

—Roxana Huebscher, PhD, RN, NP and Professor Emeritus, UW Oshkosh

How Steve Became

RALPH

A Cancer/Stem Cell Odyssey
(With Jokes)

Steve Buechler

Green Bay, WI 54311

Publishing Editor: Brittiany Koren
Copy-editor: C.M. DuPuy
Cover Art Designer: Sunny Fassbender
Interior Layout Designer: Amanda Dix

Category: Nonfiction-Cancer/Stem Cell Memoir
Description: *A Minnesota man writes to his family about his cancer diagnosis and stem cell treatment.*
Hardcover ISBN: 978-1-7335034-1-9
Paperback ISBN: 978-1-7335034-2-6
Ebook ISBN: 978-1-7335034-3-3
LOCN: Catalog info applied for.
First Edition published by Written Dreams Publishing in December, 2018.

Green Bay, WI 54311

Note to Readers

When I was diagnosed with a lethal blood cancer, I was inundated with clinical, technical information about my disease and its prognosis. But what I didn't have was an intimate, personal account of what it might be like to persevere and survive the ordeal. One goal in writing this book is to provide such an account to other patients, as well as their family members, friends, and caregivers. My story also offers medical providers a glimpse into the inner journey patients experience while under their care. And if you have managed to avoid the medical system as patient or practitioner, I offer the book as a cautionary tale and a compendium of some pretty awful jokes.

*"The ill person who turns illness into story
transforms fate into experience…"*

—Arthur Frank, from *The Wounded Storyteller*

Contents

Steve Buechler

This book is dedicated to Dr. Rachel Lerner and the doctors and nurses of the oncology ward at Methodist Hospital in St. Louis Park, Minnesota and to Dr. Nelli Bejanyan and the doctors and nurses of the Blood and Marrow Transplant Unit at the University of Minnesota Medical Center in Minneapolis, Minnesota. Their combined efforts saved my life, and this book is merely a symbolic down payment on a debt that I will never be able to fully repay.

Preface: Lessons Learned

"People tell stories not just to work out their own changing identities, but also to guide others who will follow them."
—Arthur Frank, from *The Wounded Storyteller*

Much to my surprise, some routine lab work in the spring of 2016 revealed I had abnormally low white blood cell counts. My doctor referred me to a hematologist who recommended a bone marrow biopsy. I followed their advice but was not overly concerned because I had been in good health my entire life and had no symptoms. Given that history, it was hard to imagine that any serious illness was present.

My biopsy was on a Monday. The next day, I swam my normal fifty laps, saw a chiropractor, did some shopping, and ate dinner out. On Wednesday morning, I played in my weekly poker game with some retired guys and lost ten bucks when my eighty-year-old nemesis knocked me out of the tournament. It was the last time my life would feel normal for a very long time.

That afternoon, I was informed by phone that I had acute myeloid leukemia. On Thursday, I was admitted to a hospital. On Friday, I started chemotherapy. In a mere 48 hours, I went from feeling perfectly healthy to a week-long, 24/7, chemotherapy drip.

As if that was not surreal enough, the next day my wife was admitted to the same hospital with what proved to be a fractured femur. She underwent surgery to repair her leg, spent seven days in "our" hospital, and then was discharged to a transitional care unit for another three and a half weeks. We came to think of this time as our "month from hell," though its ramifications would play out for many months thereafter.

When it became apparent that our home would be un-occupied for a month or more, I sent an email to a small group of neighbors to inform them of our status and ask them to pick up our mail and newspapers and keep an eye on our house.

I quickly realized that this was an efficient way to keep not only neighbors but family, friends, and colleagues informed about our status.

Within a couple weeks, the list of email recipients grew to a dozen, then two dozen, and eventually fifty or so recipients. Over the succeeding weeks and months, these missives grew to over sixty reports detailing my cancer odyssey.

These reports were composed for a known audience. I was highly conscious that I was writing for others, and I deliberately included some wit and humor to lighten the impact of my otherwise dire news. One of the great benefits of writing for others was the supportive feedback I received from so many of my correspondents who responded with kind words, timely advice, heartfelt prayers, and good wishes.

It eventually dawned on me that these reports had become a kind of cancer memoir consisting of serial, contemporaneous accounts of my treatment and reflections on being a cancer patient. It also occurred to me that on a more profound level, I was writing for and to myself. Each day in the hospital brought a new and dizzying array of personnel, medications, tests, scans, side-effects, cautions, and complications. While I received excellent care, it was an overwhelming initiation into the world of cancer treatment that left me feeling highly vulnerable and utterly dependent on the care of strangers.

The best way I could make sense out of it was to write about it. Writing became my therapy. It allowed me to take the chaotic, raw threads of my lived experience and weave them into a coherent, meaningful narrative of what was happening around me and *to* me.

In short, composing these reports became a psychic survival mechanism. It was many months later that it dawned on me that there could be a wider audience for the story I had been telling.

There is a vast literature advising new cancer patients about what to expect as they move from diagnosis to treatment. While valuable, this literature is both highly generic and exhaustively comprehensive. For legal and ethical reasons, it outlines every conceivable complication and side-effect of both the disease and its treatment. The unintended effect, however, can be to overwhelm the new patient, setting in motion the very depression and despair that this literature seeks to alleviate.

My story, by contrast, is uniquely personal. I make no claim to have had a typical experience. At the same time, and as my doctors endlessly repeated, there are *no* typical cases. Every cancer patient's experience is different. While unique, my story includes many experiences that may confront most cancer patients. My hope is that by reading my memoir, others will find some insight into their own stories, or those of their loved ones.

To retain the authenticity of what happened to me, I have not significantly revised or deleted any of the reports that I composed over my months of treatment and recovery. I mean to convey the immediacy of my experiences as they unfolded from day to day. The topics addressed sometimes stray into events that are not directly about my disease or treatment, but this simply illustrates how life in all its complexity does not stop just because of a life-threatening disease.

My emails periodically discuss my wife's recovery from her surgery as well as her ongoing and courageous battles with several chronic diseases that predated my own diagnosis. They also refer to an incident that preoccupied our attention at the very time I was initially hospitalized, she was recovering in a transitional care facility, and our house was unoccupied.

On July 5, 2016, a major thunderstorm swept through our neighborhood and partially downed two sixty-foot trees, damaging our roof, gutters, and deck. Within the hour, our good neighbors transmitted pictures of the damage to me in the hospital. The portion of the trees left standing posed an even greater danger to our house with more storms in the forecast, so I spent a frantic 24 hours on the phone with our tree service to take them out.

After the immediate danger had passed, I spent the next several weeks negotiating a homeowner's insurance claim from the dubious comfort of my hospital room while also weathering various complications and side-effects from my treatment. In some twisted way, I found that dealing with multiple bad things simultaneously kept me from obsessing over any one of them, and things proceeded apace. It's all part of the larger story.

On Positive Thinking

Among the responses to my reports, several people gave me credit for having a "positive attitude." It is, of course, a mainstay of the cancer literature that a positive attitude is important, if not essential to a successful outcome. I never quite understood, however, what that means beyond the clichés and bromides about keeping one's spirits up, looking on the bright side, and the like. More unsettling was the extreme versions of the positive thinking gospel that encourage patients to see their cancer as some kind of opportunity, or in the saltier language of my lady chaplain, an "AFGE." That is, another fucking growth experience.

My reservations about the positive thinking gospel had originated with Barbara Ehrenreich's *Bright-Sided: How Positive Thinking is Undermining America*. She cites credible research that positive thinking does not in fact lead to more positive outcomes. Even more importantly, it can have serious, if unintended, negative outcomes. For one, the constant encouragement to remain upbeat robs the patient of the opportunity to express their fears, despair, or disappointments as "too negative" and thus harmful to the prospects of recovery. And if they don't recover, there is the not so subtle implication that if only they had been *more* positive the outcome would have been better.

This seems like an unnecessarily cruel version of blaming the victim for outcomes that, in all likelihood, are beyond their control.

For those who know me well, the attribution of a positive attitude is a bit ironic. It's true that on the surface I am an upbeat person. I arise most every day looking forward to what life has to offer and whatever activities fill each day. Just beneath the surface, however, I have a different disposition. For most of my life, I've spent much time and energy obsessing about the future. In clinical terms, my standard operating procedure includes what therapists call "generalized anxiety."

The most trivial events can supply grist for this mill. If I have a cross-town appointment, I will think "if I leave now and traffic is light, I will arrive early and have to kill time" *but* "if I wait ten minutes and traffic is heavy, I will be late," and that is an even worse outcome. Despite these worries, I almost always arrive on time. As soon as I do, however, some new issue arises to fuel the anxiety machine. My basic programming seeks to anticipate the worst-case scenario in the hopes that I can somehow avoid, control, or sidestep every undesirable outcome.

In my rational moments, I realize that the worst-case scenario is highly unlikely to unfold, and that I am unable to control most of what happens. I've even toyed with the idea of deliberately envisioning the best-case scenario instead. It is no more likely to happen than the worst-case scenario, but at least it's a more pleasant way to pass the time. Nonethelesss, the anxiety machine remains my default mode.

You'd think that for someone with these psychological propensities, receiving a cancer diagnosis would be like throwing red meat to a pride of lions. The uncertainty and fear that such a diagnosis can trigger would seem to provide endless fuel for the anxiety machine. And yet, somehow, my diagnosis provoked an opposite response. Cancer somehow seemed too big to fit into the normal workings of the anxiety machine. Call it shock, numbness, or denial, but the diagnosis didn't provoke my standard anxiety response.

I realized there is a much better explanation for the calm attitude with which I received my diagnosis and weathered my treatment. Several months before my diagnosis, my wife and I were working on a grand plan for me to retire, for us to sell our home in Minnesota, and move to the southwest to a more hospitable climate. This would've been the most ambitious move we had ever made. We would be leaving familiar social networks and support systems for a new environment. Along the way, her ongoing health issues could pose additional challenges to our plan.

These prospects provided high octane fuel for my anxiety machine, leading to sleepless nights and endless ruminations about all the things that could go wrong. I tried sleeping pills and therapy sessions, but they didn't help much. Then, in a purely fortuitous fashion, I got a flyer in the mail announcing a six-week community education class on meditation and mindfulness.

On Mindfulness

Hoping to tame the anxiety machine, I enrolled in the class. I realized quickly that these ideas and practices were not completely unfamiliar to me. I had taken a yoga class some twenty years ago, and still had a cassette tape of mindfulness instructions. I also re-read Jon Kabat-Zinn's classic nonfiction book, *Full Catastrophe Living*. Despite this previous familiarity with yoga and mindfulness, I had never systematically integrated them into my daily life. With the anxiety machine running overtime, I decided it was time to do so.

There are many good sources on these topics, but Kabat-Zinn's work was especially helpful to me. He is widely known for pointing out that we only have moments to live. Most of us hope for many such moments, but the point is you can only live one moment at a time.

Mindfulness involves bringing a full, non-judgmental awareness to each moment as it occurs, and realizing that everything else—ruminating about the past or worrying about the future—is just noise that detracts us from our experience. This was the right message at the right time for me. The trifecta of Kabat-Zinn's book, the mindfulness class and establishing a regular yoga routine triggered a subtle but powerful change in my psychological orientation. It was not arduous or time-consuming. I simply set aside some time each day to focus on my breathing, center my awareness, and flow through yoga poses at my own pace. In addition to formal meditation or yoga, I learned I could be mindful during any activity, no matter how trivial.

The practice of mindfulness convinced me that life is not only about *what* I experience but *how* I experience it. To live mindfully is to see, taste, hear, smell, touch, and intuit even the most mundane aspects of life as rich, full, and vibrant; it's as if everything is being broadcast in high definition. This mind-set has enhanced my appreciation of simple pleasures, deepened my gratitude for the good things in my life, and enriched my empathy for others dealing with life's difficulties. Some people acquire these "benefits" as a by-product of having cancer or some other life-threatening disease. In my case, these seeds were germinating well before my diagnosis, although facing the disease and weathering its treatment brought them into full bloom.

It's more than coincidental that after a couple months of practicing mindfulness, I received my cancer diagnosis with a quiet calmness. It was as if my new routines were training me for something I didn't even know was coming. So rather than cancer being too big to fit into the anxiety machine, it's as if the machine itself had been dismantled.

If I can claim any credit for my relatively smooth course of treatment and recovery, it's due to what I learned about the practice of mindfulness. If this qualifies as "positive thinking," so be it, but the term "mindfulness" is a more precise descriptor of what sustained me through the rough times.

I practiced mindfulness, meditation, and yoga throughout my treatment, and continue to do so. Here's one example. On the day I was admitted to the hospital, things were hectic, with delays, uncertainties, and a parade of people coming into my room to introduce themselves and describe their role in my care. That evening, I distracted myself with a baseball game on television, but eventually the time came for lights out. It was then that I expected the demons to come and fill my mind with all sorts of dire possibilities.

Before that could happen, I began a meditative technique called a body scan. While lying in bed, I took half a dozen slow, deep cleansing breaths. I focused all my awareness on my toes and any sensations I could detect there. I slowly moved my awareness to my feet, ankles, and lower legs. Ten minutes later, as I was trying to focus on my torso, I fell into a peaceful sleep.

I repeated this process for the next month, until I realized I could fall asleep without resorting to the body scan. While I lost plenty of sleep when the night shift came into my room to check vital signs, draw blood, administer medications, or empty trash cans (really? at 4 am?), I never lost sleep ruminating about how my disease and its treatment would play out.

On Being Pro-Active

My psychological makeup includes an excessive need for control in a wide variety of situations. I do not think I have banished this need for control to the same extent that I have transcended the anxiety machine. But being more mindful has tempered my impulse for control in some beneficial ways.

Now, when the control impulse arises, I pause to consider the immediate situation before me. I ask myself what I can control, if anything, and whether I need to do so at all. Knowing this was especially beneficial during my initial thirty-seven-day hospital stay. I was keenly aware that my world had become very small, and that even within that small world, there was little I could control.

Accepting those parameters, I focused on what I could control. I made a point of making my hospital bed each morning and keeping my room tidy and organized. I established a regimen of stretching, physical therapy, and a lot of hall-walking while trailing my IV pole behind me. I even mastered yoga poses, including the downward dog, while receiving chemotherapy infusions. I just had to make sure my tubing was long enough to provide freedom of motion. It became my way of saying that while I may be stuck here, I can still be an active agent in at least some of what happens while I'm here.

I also sought to be pro-actively involved in my care to the greatest possible extent. I don't know if my attitude was "positive" as much as it was practical. I used each daily visit with my doctors to clarify where we were at, what I could expect, and what I might do to further my recovery. I asked questions about test results, medication changes, new symptoms, and possible side-effects, and my doctors patiently responded to all my queries. My treatment came to feel like a collaborative project that blended their expertise, my experience, and our mutual willingness to solve problems.

Cancer treatment is rooted in science, but it also draws on a doctor's training, craft, and experience. While patients may not grasp all the nuances of the science, their input can nonetheless complement a doctor's skills and inform their judgments and recommendations. It was only through collaborative conversation that my doctors and I identified one drug (among so many) that caused me to have a nasty full-body rash. They switched out that drug and the rash gradually disappeared. On another occasion, I traced an unpleasant drug interaction effect to two medications I was taking simultaneously. When I proposed changing the dosing schedule, they concurred, and the problem was resolved.

As any hospital patient knows, while doctors are crucial to one's care, they tend to drop in at unpredictable times for brief visits. It is the nurses who become a patient's most frequent contacts during a hospital stay, and I was determined to cultivate positive relations with the nurses who cared for me. It helped that while my various nurses differed in temperament and style, they were uniformly competent and compassionate. That made it easier to do my part as a "good" patient and get things off on the right foot.

When time permitted, the nurses and I might chat about relatives, crack some jokes, commiserate about politics, or share life stories. Each of these conversations reframed their clinical care-giving into a more human and personal interaction. The small efforts I made to establish rapport were repaid many times over in the care I received. More than any other factor, my relationships with my nurses were the most positive and memorable aspects of my hospital stays.

As one example, I remember walking the halls one day, turning a corner, and seeing three of my favorite nurses consulting about another patient. Given all they had done for me, the mere sight of them together brought a powerful wave of emotion and not a few tears. And yes, before I was discharged, I told them just how important they had become to me.

On Humor

To be sure, cancer is no laughing matter. That is precisely why I found it essential to retain my sense of humor upon my diagnosis and throughout my treatment. Doing so became an antidote to the somber reality of what I was facing. It became a quiet form of resistance that kept the cancer at arm's length for me. In my mind, having a sense of humor was a way of saying you may make me sick and eventually may kill me, but I'm still going to enjoy a good (or bad) joke.

An early lesson I learned about the importance of humor that has always resonated with me is from a scene in the film *Hannah and Her Sisters*. Woody Allen plays a hypochondriac fearing that he is dying from a brain tumor. (Spoiler alert) When he receives a clean bill of health, he is elated, but only momentarily. He realizes that someday he will die of something. In classic Allen fashion, he ponders why life is even worth living if we are all going to die anyway. In this melancholy mood on a brisk, blustery day, he prowls the Upper West Side of Manhattan for hours with no apparent purpose.

In an almost random fashion, he buys a ticket at a movie theater and sits down in the middle of a Marx Brothers movie. After watching for a while, he has a revelation and realizes that even though we may never be able to answer the big existential questions about life, death, mortality, or evil, any world that includes the Marx Brothers is a world worth living in. As if to prove this point, the movie's last scene is uncharacteristically upbeat.

Upon its 1986 release, I had been trying to secure a tenure-track, professorial position for four years while surviving on one-year contracts at an institution whose budget for my position had run out. When I had just about given up hope, I received and accepted my one and only tenure-track offer, which launched me on a lifelong academic career. My happy ending paralleled that in Allen's film, and solidified my appreciation for its message about the importance of humor in dire times.

My sense of humor is wide-ranging, from the wacky antics of the Marx Brothers and Monty Python to the cerebral musings of George Carlin and Steven Wright to the political satire of Stephen Colbert and Bill Maher. But in the following reports, my stock in trade are jokes that rely on corny puns, double entendre, and non-sequiturs. They are as likely to produce a groan as a guffaw, but it's all good to me.

In my initial email to our neighbors letting them know of our predicament, I concluded with a joke to lighten the mood. I wanted to indicate that despite the near simultaneous shock of my cancer diagnosis and my wife Sue's broken leg, my sense of humor was still intact. This afterthought quickly morphed into the "Joke of the Day" as a regular feature in my emails. Some recipients held their nose and advised me not to quit my day job; others said they liked them and to keep them coming; and still others began to supply me with jokes when the well was running dry. So, to repeat: while cancer *is* no laughing matter, maintaining a sense of humor became a critical survival tool for me.

It would be presumptuous of me to give advice to others embarking on their own cancer treatment, but these are the practices that helped me. My recipe combined support from family, friends, and email correspondents; mindfulness, meditation, and yoga; a proactive approach to my treatment; good communication with doctors and nurses; and an unrelenting sense of humor. This combination allowed me to make the best of a bad situation.

On Faith and Secularism

My parents were nominal Catholics and I was raised in that tradition. I was baptized, took first Communion, was confirmed, and attended Sunday Mass with my family into my early teens. With the onset of puberty and a teenager's classic sense of immortality, Catholicism lost its relevance. I fell away from a religion I had never fully embraced.

After drifting through my teenage years, I enrolled in college and became enamored with philosophy and sociology. I found their emphasis on scientific observation, logical reasoning, and rational explanation to be much more compelling. I became a "child" of the Enlightenment and a secular humanist. This stress on reason, however, has a dark side that academics call instrumental rationality. This debased form reduces it to a tool that can serve any goal. Hence, the same scientific, instrumental rationality that drives medical research to save lives can also be used to develop more lethal weaponry that takes lives away. The thin boundary between chemotherapy and chemical warfare is an example of how closely related these uses can be.

As powerful as it may be, rationality must be tempered with morality if it is to lead to humane outcomes. This has been one of the historic roles of religion, but it isn't the only basis for morality. It's also possible to derive moral values from the secular tradition.

One of the best examples is Philip Zuckerman's *Living the Secular Life: New Answers to Old Questions*. In the early stages of my treatment, a colleague suggested I read this book. As I did, it resonated strongly with my own views.

One of Zuckerman's observations was that secular-minded people may weather challenges such as a life-threatening illness more readily than someone who is religious. For the latter, such an event may precipitate a crisis of faith and a quest to restore that faith while dealing with their illness. For the secular-minded, there is no crisis because there was no ultimate faith to be shaken in the first place.

This could allow secular-minded folks to more readily adopt a pragmatic, problem-solving attitude toward life's misfortunes. It certainly resonates with the pro-active stance that I brought to my treatment. Whenever possible, I sought to act and solve problems in ways that would foster my recovery. When it wasn't possible, I learned new levels of patience and acceptance from my practice of mindfulness.

This was my frame of mind when I received a visit from a hospital chaplain who asked if I wanted to talk about my circumstances. My own stereotype of a chaplain is a stern, dour, old Bible-thumping man. Instead I faced an upbeat, fashionably-dressed, middle-aged woman. So much for stereotypes.

I told her that I was a committed secular humanist and didn't think we had much to discuss. She explained to me that it wasn't about what *she* believed, but what *I* believed.

That surprised me.

And it launched a series of conversations between us about spiritual beliefs, secular morality, meditation practice, emotional rollercoasters, mood swings, identity changes, and so much more. Her receptivity to my views and our ensuing discussions was a model for me of how differing belief systems can respectfully co-exist.

My beliefs allowed me to arrive at a good place during a bad time. It worked for me, but I also recognize there are as many different paths to good places as there are diverse faith traditions and belief systems. As a pragmatic matter, whatever gets someone to a good place is their business. As an ethical issue, acknowledging those varied paths—religious, spiritual, or secular—seemed the only reasonable stance I could take.

On Privilege, Care, and Support

My healing and recovery occurred in a larger context that was unusually privileged and highly favorable in several respects. My employer provided me with excellent health insurance that covered virtually all my major expenses. My longevity in my position earned me a year of paid sick leave, covering the period from the onset of my disease to my retirement date.

After retiring, I maintained a version of this same good health insurance and began receiving a significant pension. I had the good fortune to not have to worry about financial constraints on the decisions I made and the care I received. (My privilege *should be* everyone's right in an "advanced," industrial nation, but that's a whole other talk show.)

There was an interpersonal aspect that worked in my

favor as well. As a highly educated, professional white male, I was taken seriously and treated respectfully by everyone I encountered. When I responded in kind, all my interactions with medical personnel were congenial and productive. This helped give me the confidence to be my own advocate.

My self-advocacy reminded me of a friend (who is a registered nurse) who believes *every* hospital patient needs an advocate to represent their needs while navigating the complexities of hospital care. If they are unable to play this role themselves, a caregiver advocate should be assigned to them.

Another positive factor was the quality of care that I received throughout my treatment within two major hospitals. There were, of course, too many forms to complete, some silly bureaucratic impediments, and some truly awful hospital food. But when it came to the important things, the care I received was superb. My doctors and nurses consistently combined skill and expertise with compassion and empathy in ways I will never forget or could ever repay. Suffice it to say, my stereotypical views of the medical profession have been forever transformed into a profound appreciation.

Alongside that care, it would be impossible to overstate the benefits of the social support I received from my spouse, relatives, friends, neighbors, and colleagues. Through their hospital visits, phone calls, emails, get-well cards, gifts, and the key lime pie my wife and her sister smuggled into my room, I was continually reminded of how many people were pulling for me, praying for me, thinking of me, and sending me positive vibes.

I am deeply grateful for my privileged status, excellent care, and social support. And I'm acutely aware that others without my privileges may not receive the same level of care. For me, these privileges made it much easier to implement the pro-active strategies described above. But the inequalities of privilege are also a reminder that however much we may try to control our destiny, outcomes are always intertwined with larger forces beyond our control.

Steve Buechler

On Medical Miracles and Luck

C. Wright Mills famously described the sociological imagination as a means to understand how individual lives are shaped by larger social forces. These forces include social structure, or how our position in society can bring privileges and disadvantages that influence the course of our lives. This also includes historical location, or how each generation encounters new opportunities and constraints as they create their individual biographies.

While my education and career granted me a favorable position in the social structure, my parents also picked a good time to bring me into the world. As a baby boomer, I lived into my sixties before contracting a life-threatening disease—acute myeloid leukemia—that was incurable throughout much of the 20th century. I am humbled by the fact that the procedure that saved my life has only been available for a couple of decades.

The first successful bone marrow transplant occurred in 1968 at the University of Minnesota Hospital. In the early 1980s, the first bone marrow donor registries were established, but as of 1986 only about 5,000 transplants had been performed worldwide. The next advance came when French researchers transplanted stem cells from umbilical cord blood in 1988. The first successful cord blood transplant in the US followed in 1995. The Blood and Marrow Transplant Unit at the University of Minnesota Medical Center has since become a leader in umbilical cord blood research and transplants. In the fifteen years before my diagnosis, they performed almost 1,000 such transplants and were routinely achieving successful outcomes.

As a beneficiary of this scientific progress, my procedure began with a week of "conditioning." It's a pleasant-sounding term for high dose chemotherapy and full body radiation to destroy virtually all my diseased bone marrow and white blood cells. That paved the way for a genetically matched, double umbilical cord blood transplant. The "transplant" is not a conventional, surgical intervention; it is simply a transfusion of donor blood that introduces new stem cells into the body.

Once there, the stem cells just "know" where to go to begin producing new bone marrow and all the other cells needed for a healthy immune system. The reason for *two* cord blood sources instead of one was to double the chances of successful engraftment. The cords came from one of the donor banks that had only been established in recent decades. As a bonus, I live less than thirty miles from the University of Minnesota Medical Center whose personnel pioneered this technique, performed my transplant, and provided follow-up care, making me part of the first generation to have access to this procedure. In Mills's language, my social position and generational timing may have been beyond my control, but they both worked in my favor.

Speaking of forces beyond our control, there is also having pure good luck. As a poker player, I have often pondered the parallels between the vagaries of poker and the vicissitudes of life. In both, we must make decisions with incomplete and imperfect information, and the stakes can be quite high. If we draw on our rationality and intuition, we can assess the risks, calculate the odds, check our gut, and make the best decision at the time. In the case of my procedure, the "house" was offering me odds any poker player would relish, but the downside was a 15-20% mortality rate from the procedure itself. So, you "win" at least 80% of the time. Otherwise, it's game over.

That sobering scenario led me to take my time, do my homework, examine my options, get second opinions, and reach a measured decision to go ahead with the procedure. As good as such decisions may be, however, outcomes in poker and life are still subject to unpredictable and unknowable factors. For all our pro-active efforts to control outcomes, it's healthy to retain some humility in a universe that can still roll dice with our fate.

On the Title

Naming confers meaning onto experience and is not to be taken lightly. Early on, I characterized my treatment as a "journey," but that never felt quite right. After reading other cancer memoirs, I came to see the term as an over-used cliché. The word connotes a degree of choice, a sense of adventure, the prospect of pleasure, and a known destination that are foreign to cancer treatment. I've been through a noteworthy experience, but "journey" does not capture it.

Perhaps the most over-used metaphor about cancer sees it as a war in which the heroic patient valiantly battles an evil foe. This also did not ring true for me. For starters, we have enough militarized aspects of life without extending the imagery to illness. This metaphor also concedes too much to cancer. It is not a conscious, willful antagonist. Cancer is just a biological process originating from within the body that simply is what it is and does what it does. And although I felt like many things throughout my treatment, heroic warrior or combat victim were not amongst them.

These particular thoughts led me to use the term "odyssey." When I ran it by my longtime colleague, Tom, he captured the rationale more eloquently than I ever could. He wrote back to me.

You are right about the connotation that it is less volitional, especially in the sense that events beyond your control (fate, and potentially fatal events) forced this journey. The word also has a stronger connotation of a learned quest in conjunction with those unforeseeable hardships and uncertain outcomes. And the fact that your story is in large part one of science and new medical developments is a good fit with the ancient Greek allusion, Greek being the core linguistic basis of medical terminology. Through the same logic, the term also works well with the secular angle.

Nicely put, Tom. I always knew you were a smart guy.

As for the name of the main title, it was set in motion on a sunny August afternoon between chemotherapy treatments when I received an important phone call from the University of Minnesota Blood and Marrow Transplant Unit. They informed me that, based on genetic testing of my cancer, they had found promising umbilical cord blood matches for me. That provided the green light to proceed with the transplant.

As my transplant day drew near, I became curious about my donors. All I could learn was that the cords were from an infant boy and girl. Since I was going to have a rather intimate relationship with these kids, I playfully named them "Ralph" and "Gwen."

Three weeks after the transplant, a bone marrow biopsy confirmed that one of the cords was 99% engrafted, which was unusually early for a cord blood procedure. The biopsy also revealed that the stem cells that had engrafted were from Ralph. To outward appearances, I remain the same person I've always been. At the cellular level, however, I am a fundamentally different person with new DNA to boot. Thus, while I still feel like "Steve," in an important biological sense, this is the story of how Steve became Ralph.

The Odyssey: From Diagnosis and Treatment to Recovery and Survival
1. Induction Chemotherapy and Hospitalization
(What the Hell is Going on Here?)

"What story do you wish to tell of yourself? How will you shape your illness, and yourself, in the stories you tell of it?"
—Arthur Frank, from *The Wounded Storyteller*

The following reports were composed during my initial 37-day hospital stay between mid-June and late July of 2016. That stay began with a week of "induction" chemotherapy, but the whole experience was an *induction* into the world of hospital procedures and protocols that were all new to me. I was fortunate to have some terrific nurses who were reliable guides throughout this unfamiliar terrain.

This was also the time when I was most preoccupied with my wife's own medical challenges, as well as the storm damage to our home. As a result, these issues loomed large in my early correspondence with neighbors, family, and friends.

Family Medical Update
(file under "not so good" news)
June 23, 2016

Hi All,

Last week I received some shocking medical news, and I want to keep our closer neighbors accurately informed about the situation. For now, I'd prefer that you keep this amongst the recipients of this list until I know a bit more about where this is going.

Doctors have been monitoring a slow decline in my white blood cells for a couple years, but the decline became more drastic in the last couple months. A bone marrow biopsy last Monday revealed cancer cells, and I was notified Wednesday, hospitalized Thursday, and began chemotherapy on Friday.

The shocking part is that I had been completely asymptomatic, swimming 50 laps every other day and going about my business as a healthy person until I got the call that I am apparently quite ill.

The diagnosis is acute myeloid leukemia. The treatment is seven days of a cocktail of two chemo drugs in the hospital, followed by another three weeks in the hospital for monitoring and controlling infections that inevitably will follow in the wake of carpet bombing my red and white blood cells, platelets, and bone marrow. (Did you know chemotherapy is a derivative of the chemical warfare deployed in WWI?)

If it goes well, I can leave the hospital for a while. However, this is a cancer that returns often, so there will be a follow-up treatment. Based on pending genetic testing of the cancer cells, that could be more chemo or a stem cell transplant.

Does this sound a bit surreal? But wait, there's more.

Last Friday as I started chemo, Sue was admitted to the same hospital with a hairline fracture in her right leg—the femur bone—as a side effect of long-term steroid use to control her chronic inflammation. Her femur needed to have hardware surgically implanted before it became a full-blown broken leg. Her operation was Tuesday the 21st, and it went well, with a small twist. As they installed the hardware to stabilize the hairline fracture, the "fracture completed" so she ended up with a "broken leg." This is a routine outcome as they install the hardware, which will now do the job of holding the leg together for healing with no need for a cast. If the leg had fully broken before surgery, it would've been a much tougher repair and recovery.

Sue already took some small steps the day after surgery and is probably looking at a couple days of physical therapy in the hospital before going to a transitional care unit for a couple of weeks. She should have a room at her previous TCU, which is by far the best of the three she has been in over the last 18 months.

We're very grateful for our developing support team. My brother, Jerome came up for the weekend from Wisconsin, and Sue's sister, Jan is here in town. She will be staying some nights at our house and keeping us supplied with vital items from there. The burgundy Buick LaCrosse you may occasionally see in our driveway belongs to her.

Joyce (neighbor extraordinaire) has graciously agreed to collect our mail and newspapers for Sue's sister to bring to us, and ever-reliable and unfailingly cheerful Andrew has been recruited to mow our lawn.

We will see how things play out when we return home,

but it gives me great comfort to be living in such a friendly and congenial neighborhood where people have been so supportive through Sue's earlier medical challenges.

Having said all that, I think I'm doing remarkably well so far. I'm tolerating the chemo, have no infections, complications or significant side-effects yet, have good care, and I am working on mindfulness, meditation, yoga, and as much physical activity as my circumstances will allow. I'm told it will get uglier next week when my immunity bottoms out, but one thing at a time, eh?

Thanks for reading this far; I'll be in touch as I get more information about how this is going to play out.

Optimistically,
Steve

P. S. Medical joke of the day (for those of you who appreciate a really corny joke):

Three vampires walk into a bar. The bartender says, "What are you boys having?"

The first vampire says, "I'll have a blood."

The second vampire says, "Me, too."

The third vampire says, "Make mine a plasma."

The bartender says, "Let me get this straight: that's two bloods and a blood light, right?"

News Flash: Sue Gets Time Off for Good Behavior
June 24, 2016

Hi All,

I just wanted to let everyone know that Sue and her re-paired femur were discharged to an excellent transitional care unit that she stayed in last November while recovering from a pulmonary embolism. Some of the excellent staff recognized her upon arrival and are helping her get settled in, even as I write this.

All things considered, this is absolutely the best place for her to be right now. We were delighted that they had the space and she made a smooth transfer over there. She may well be looking at a couple weeks of rehab before returning home, but that's what she needs to be safe in our house.

Meanwhile, my appeal to leave fell on deaf ears and I must stay in the hospital. All things considered, that's also the best thing, given what's coming. As my immunity bottoms out, they need to monitor and fight the inevitable infections.

Joke of the Day (*imagine a termite with a clipped, British accent for greater effect*):

A termite walks into a bar where three vampires are enjoying their bloods and blood lite.

The termite approaches the vampires and says, "Excuse me, can you tell me? Is the bar tender here?"

Cheers,
Steve

Update on Steve and Sue
June 28, 2016

Hi All,

With apologies for trying to update a lot of people at one time, here goes.

My smooth trip through seven days of chemo encountered a not unexpected infection over the weekend as I got to dance with a gal named E. coli. Apparently, she's been in my gut my whole life but never had a chance to kick up her heels till my immunity was destroyed by the chemo. It was an ugly 36 hours, but the 3 prophylactic antibiotics I was already on, plus a new one, have tamed the fever and alleviated most of the symptoms. Do let me know, however, if you have any good adult diaper jokes.

My platelets have also dropped as expected, so I signed a consent form this morning for them to give me a platelet transfusion to aid clotting in the event of serious bleeding. Of course, I could have refused, in which case they wait for you to have serious bleeding first and then treat you with…a platelet transfusion.

Sue's adventure continues at her TCU. Apparently, the level of care is not quite as good as her last stay, but they are working on better communication. The physical and occupational therapy will allow her to go home safely and in a timely fashion.

Thanks to those of you who have sent cards or emails thus far. Twisted humor is especially welcome, as epitomized by my long-time friend Dave from Milwaukee, whose card proclaims something like people who think laughter is the best medicine apparently have never had morphine.

On that note, let's close with a joke.

Joke of the Day:

A grasshopper walks into a bar recently vacated by vampires. Before he can order, the bartender exclaims "This is amazing—we have a drink named after you."

The grasshopper looks perplexed, furrows his brow, and then says, "Why would anyone name a drink 'Melvin'?"

Bonus alternate version: A screwdriver walks into a bar, etc.

Cheers,
Steve

Favorite Joke
June 29, 2016

Hi All,

I'm getting more platelets today and feeling healthier and stronger…but on to the important stuff.

I saw Garrison Keillor being interviewed on television today and he was asked what is his favorite joke. Given his retirement from Prairie Home Companion and his expertise as the author of the "Pretty Good Joke Book," I pass on his favorite joke.

A man is walking by an insane asylum and hears a rhythmic chant repeating "21, 21, 21" coming from the main building. Unable to contain his curiosity, he approaches the building and looks in the window.

Just then a patient reaches through the bars and stabs the man in the eye with a sharp object. As he falls to the ground and loses consciousness, he hears the chant "22, 22, 22."

Cheers,
Steve

Some Upcoming Medical Turning Points (and a serialized joke!)
June 30, 2016

Hi All,

Within a few days, I expect some important test results that will shape my ongoing treatment. I'll outline the possibilities here. If you ever want more information on this stuff, email or call me directly. By the same token, if you'd prefer to opt out of future emails, just let me know.

Short term issues:

I was initially diagnosed with leukemia through a bone marrow biopsy on June 13, leading to hospitalization and a seven-day chemo regimen that began on June 17. Today, I had a follow-up bone marrow biopsy to assess the effectiveness of the chemo treatment. The results won't be in for a couple days, but there are two basic possibilities.

First, it may show no cancer cells detectable by this method at this time. If so, I will remain in the hospital for two plus weeks to monitor/treat any additional infections while my blood counts recover to the point where I can be safely discharged into the big world for a month or so. This is the expected outcome based on how other patients have responded to this chemo regimen.

Second, it may show remaining cancer cells, in which case they will resume chemo and assess with another biopsy. This will obviously add to my time in the hospital, but they won't let me go until I'm in "remission," as measured by a bone marrow biopsy.

Long term issues:

Because this cancer returns often, there will be a second stage of treatment. The tissue from my first biopsy is still being analyzed to reveal the genetic composition of the cancer cells. These results will take a bit more time, but again, there are two basic possibilities.

First, if the cancer is judged to be "less risky," the follow-up will involve a different chemo regimen starting sometime after my month at home to rest and recover. This should not involve long-term hospitalization but could require shorter stays of a few days at a time.

Second, if the cancer is judged to be "more risky," the recommended follow-up is a stem cell transplant. This is a longer, more intensive, higher risk/reward treatment that would take place either at the U. of M. or the Mayo Clinic.

Meanwhile, this is day 15 for me and I have had only one identifiable chemo-induced infection: the E. coli bacteria, which responded well to treatment after a couple of bad days. My only other issue is a rash that is probably an allergic reaction to any one of four antibiotics I have been on. They are going to change the antibiotic regimen to still control E. coli (and other nasties), but allow the rash to disappear. The consensus is that I'm doing well and have weathered what they anticipated as the worst week in really good shape. I look forward to more weeks of getting healthier and stronger, which will serve me well in the next stage.

Sue's situation has stabilized for the better, with several RNs and a social worker helping to smooth out some initial bumps in the road. As her surgical wound continues to heal, she can move into a more active phase of physical and occupational therapy in preparation for a return home.

As a reward for reading this far, we have a new feature in the form of a serial joke in three parts. We hope you enjoy it.

Serial Joke Part 1:
An unlikely trio are walking down the street together: a ham sandwich, a string, and a pair of jumper cables. As they turn a corner, they see a bar. In rather juvenile fashion, they dare each other to go in and see if they can get served. The ham sandwich takes the initiative, so...

A ham sandwich walks into a bar. The bartender sees him immediately, holds up his hands, and says "I'm sorry, but you will have to leave. We don't serve food here."

Cheers,
Steve

Waiting Game
July 2, 2016

Hi All,

Two different oncology consultants have led me to believe that I would have the results of my Thursday bone marrow biopsy by today and know whether the chemo has worked or not.

This morning I had a visit from a third oncologist, a Dr. Debbie Downer, who sang a different tune. She said it could take up to a week to perform all the secondary tests with the biopsied tissue and arrive at a definitive answer as to whether I am "cancer-free" now or whether I will need additional rounds of chemo to reach that goal.

I also mentioned to her a recurring headache over the last few days, and Debbie did not hesitate to outline the most gruesome (if extremely remote) possibilities for me. To explore it further, they have scheduled a CT scan for 9 PM tonight. It's hardly the first time that someone has told me I need to have my head examined, so we'll see how it ranks with other fun Saturday night activities.

For those of you keeping score on my immuno-suppressed infections and complications, the colitis and E. coli are on the run (no pun intended), the skin rash is under active investigation, and the headaches await further testing.

Sue and I talk daily and compare notes on my care here and her experience at the transitional care unit. She arrived at the unit with a surgically repaired right femur eight days ago, and the wound site continued to seep for several days. That delayed the start of the physical therapy, but that has now commenced, and they will rehabilitate her to the point where she can safely return home.

Meanwhile, several people have expressed interest in the next installment of the serial joke of the week, with one intrepid correspondent even attempting to guess (unsuccessfully) the next punchline. Since several other people are new to this mailing list, you should know that in part one of our serial joke, a ham sandwich was denied entry to a bar because they do not "serve food." On we go.

Serial Joke Part 2:
As the dejected ham sandwich takes a seat on the curb, the string decides to try his luck at gaining entry to the bar. So...

A string walks in to a bar.

The bartender sees him and immediately says "I'm sorry, but you will have to leave. We don't serve strings here."

The string leaves but does not give up. He decides on a disguise. He twists his body into a loop, stands tall and erect, and tousles his hair into a spiky, punk look. He re-enters the bar.

The bartender is suspicious and says "Hey, you look a little like that string I just kicked out of here, but I can't be sure, so I have to ask: are you a string?"

The string looks him straight in the eye and calmly responds, "No sir, I'm afraid not."

Cheers,
Steve

Waiting Game Part 2
July 3, 2016

Hi All,

Today brings mostly good but somewhat inconclusive news.

Last night, I had a CT scan of my head to help diagnose a persistent morning headache. The report is in and it's official: they found nothing in my head…er…nothing that shouldn't be there, that is. So, there is no infection, cancer, or hemorrhage going on there. After this incredibly high-tech scanning process and consultation between several doctors, the upshot is that maybe I should try a decongestant.

Then, I had a second meeting with Dr. Debbie Downer. I now think I may have been a bit unfair to her. Today she displayed a better bedside manner and the discussion was very informative, if highly technical, so let's rename her Dr. Debbie Detail.

The bone marrow biopsy report has come back. This was to determine whether cancer is still present or not after chemo and the result is…inconclusive. So now we'll redo the bone marrow biopsy in two more weeks. By then, it should yield a definitive result. Best case: no cancer is evident, my blood cell counts are back up, and I can still go home close to the original schedule of mid-to-late July. Worst case: some cancer is still there, and we reboot the process with another round of chemo, then several weeks of recovery, and a later return home by several weeks. If I've learned anything so far, there are probably numerous possible cases in between the best and worst-case scenarios.

For my part, I'm walking the halls 3x per day for 20-30 minutes each, in addition to daily yoga. What I see on my walks is sobering. Virtually all the other patients appear much sicker and more debilitated than I feel. I am so grateful to be relatively healthy, and that my cancer does not involve the pain of other cancers that present in a particular location or organ or require heavy duty narcotics and their inevitable side-effects.

Confirming my impressions, Dr. Debbie Detail volunteered the observation that I am doing exceptionally well compared to other people, including those with my diagnosis. She credits my overall health status coming in here and said that will serve me well throughout the remainder of the process.

I also need to acknowledge the nursing staff here. Everyone has been competent, professional, and respectful, but there are at least four nurses I have nominated to my "A team." They have provided exceptional care that has gone beyond medical and technical skill by offering a more holistic level of care that touches all the emotional and psychological bases as well. They even do a convincing job of laughing at my jokes. I don't know what they are paid, but they deserve much, much more.

I'm sorry to ramble on so long but consider this my mid-term report. Sue's situation remains much the same; her leg can now bear weight and she will be gradually increasing her walking distance with each day, along with other rehabilitation exercises. For my part, I don't anticipate much hard news for a couple more weeks, and I won't bore you with every little infection or side-effect that comes along. More importantly, I don't have enough jokes to keep up daily reports. However, it is time to finish the serial joke.

Serial Joke Part 3:

Synopsis: The ham sandwich has been ejected from the bar because they don't serve food. The string has gained entry disguised as a frayed knot and is nursing a drink at the bar. This leaves only the last member of our trio, so...

A pair of jumper cables walks into a bar. The bartender spies him immediately and says in a stern voice: "Okay, look, I'll serve you, but I don't want you starting anything in here."

Cheers,
Steve

Now for Something Completely Different
July 6, 2016

Hi All,

A special welcome to the half dozen newbies who have been added to the mass mailing list. You've missed some terrible jokes of the day, but you'll be in on the rest of them.

It has occurred to me that my past communiques have

been rather narrowly focused on my and Sue's health. Important, but rather tedious after a while. Today, with deference to Monte Python's Flying Circus, it is now time for something completely different.

My neighbors already know this, but for the rest of you, there was a bit of a storm in our corner of the world last night. If a picture is worth a thousand words, I've attached two thousand words showing you what our front and back yard looked like after the storm. It's by far the worst storm damage we have had in the fifteen years we have lived in that house.

Operating from my hospital bed, I have opened a claim with our insurance company, contacted my local insurance agent, and called upon an excellent tree service company that we have used several times in the past. The city has already come by and cleared the debris that intrudes into the road, but we need the tree service to intervene and save us from any more damage.

The tree in front of the house still has a major limb that extends over the roof, but it is no longer counterbalanced by the limb that currently occupies the driveway. So now the goal is to get the tree service guys to take out the limb overhanging the house before the next storm that could bring it through the roof. A drama I don't really need, but like much of the last three weeks, I don't seem to have a lot of control over that situation.

My family had a saying that bad things come in 3s. Assuming my cancer, Sue's broken leg, and our tree situation qualify for this rule, it should be clear sailing from here. What's very heartening is the help we are getting from our neighbors. Our insurance company may have a slogan about a good neighbor, but the really good neighbors throughout this little drama have been the folks who share our shoreline on Duck Lake. Thanks so much to you all for the pictures, the multiple phone calls, the damage assessment, and the updates on everything connected to this episode.

Oh yeah, medical update. Not much to say for Sue or me except we're in a holding pattern. I still have a nasty rash that is probably a reaction to one of the seemingly countless antibiotics or anti-fungal medications they have been giving me. But my vital signs are good; I have no fever or active infection now, and my appetite and energy level remain good. I plan to retain my title as "the guy who walks the halls more than any other patient."

And so, we come to the joke.

Joke of the Day:
A horse walks into a bar and the bartender says, "Hey buddy, why the long face?"

Cheers,
Steve

"Something Completely Different"
Update
July 8, 2016

Hi All,

After a hectic couple of days on the phone and internet to our insurance company and tree service, there's some good news to report.

For over a decade, we have used a very reliable and

proficient tree service here in the Twin Cities. Long story short, less than 48 hours after the initial damage, they brought four trucks with hydraulic lift buckets and eight guys who cleared virtually all the downed trees and debris in a little over two hours.

First priority was the limb overhanging our roof from an unbalanced tree, but following our instructions, they took both trees out completely. If you've seen the "before" pictures, the attached "after" pictures make for quite a contrast. We don't have any shade and our house looks naked, but we're out of the woods (no pun intended) as far as further damage from this episode. They do great work, but the less said about the cost, the better.

Now it will be a matter of negotiating with the insurance adjustor, which isn't easy to do from a hospital bed. They should cover the damage to the deck, but it remains to be seen if there is other damage they are able to find and willing to cover.

Not much action on the medical front. I'm stuck in the hospital, so the staff can monitor and treat any infections that arise. My goal is twofold: have a good bone marrow biopsy in about ten days that shows no cancer cells and have my counts (white blood cells, red blood cells, and platelets) back up to a point where I can weather the germs out there in the real world. If so, I could leave as early as two weeks from now. If not, they'll keep me here short term for counts to improve further or long term to restart chemo, if needed.

Meanwhile, in another part of town, Sue is rehabbing her leg and starting to work on climbing just a few stairs with a cane and bannister toward the eventual goal of handling our 13 steps between the first and second floors at home.

That's it for now, except, of course, for the joke.

Joke of the Day:

A snail *tries* to enter a bar but can't reach the door handle. It knocks on the door instead. The bartender opens the door, doesn't see anyone, and is about to close the door when he looks down and sees the snail.

The snail looks up and says "Good afternoon, sir. I wonder if you would be interested in purchasing some magazine subscriptions."

Well, the bartender has had a bad day, and this is the last straw. He swings his leg back and kicks the snail as hard as he can, and the snail goes flying through the air. The bartender slams the door and goes back to work.

Two years later...

The same bartender hears a gentle knock on the door. He opens it, doesn't see anyone, is about to close it when he looks down and sees the same snail.

The snail looks up at him and asks, "So what the hell was *that* all about?"

Cheers,
Steve

Why you want Homeowner's Insurance
July 11, 2016

Hi All,

Now that the downed trees have been removed, our insurance adjustor has paid a visit to our house and found rather extensive damage. He initially said he would write a claim for the entire garage roof, the west-facing main roof, and damage to the gutters, deck, and other incidentals. The implication was that we would have to pay out-of-pocket for the east-facing main roof to complete the job and have it covered by a warranty.

The "split-roof" coverage was a new one on me, but their argument was that half the roof was not damaged and so couldn't be covered.

Twenty minutes after he left the house, he called me back and said he just "remembered" there was some damage to the east-facing main roof from some evergreens that got slammed into the roof by the north to south winds. Given that, he said they could cover the cost of the entire roof (if his superiors accept his assessment). I'm glad he recovered his memory, because that will save us whatever the going rate for half a roof is these days.

So, the next challenge is to hire a reliable, reasonably priced roofer (words rarely seen together) to do the work. My appeal to our good neighbors has already yielded several referrals, so I'll be working on those in the coming days. I also want to extend a big thanks to our neighbor for going up on our garage roof and temporarily plugging a hole that otherwise might have allowed water to accumulate on the insulation and the ceiling of the family room.

Not much new on the medical front. My platelets are recovering, which means my body is doing part of its job now that the chemo has ended its assault. However, my white blood cell count has remained very low for more than a week. I need my body to do the rest of its job and begin manufacturing those oh-so-handy white blood cells that comprise our immune system. In the last 24 hours, I have been running a medium grade fever again, so they have done a chest X-ray (negative) and requested samples of every conceivable body fluid to identify the infectious culprit. Then they'll prescribe yet another antibiotic that should be effective against it.

Sue is continuing her slow and steady progress, walking longer distances and navigating a few stairs toward the eventual goal of being able to go home safely. Last Saturday, she got a "day pass" so her sister brought her over to my hospital for a brief visit. It was the first visual contact we've had in almost three weeks. It was quite a party comparing our respective bruises, IV ports, and the all the rest.

So, this brings us to the joke.

Joke of the day:
A bear walks into a bar. The bartender asks what he's having, and the bear raises his arms, stutters and stammers, and falls silent for an extended period.

With a touch of impatience, the bartender eventually says, "Hey buddy, what's with the big pause?"

Cheers,
Steve

News: The Good, Bad, and the Ugly
July 14, 2016

Hi All,

This cancer business comes with quite a learning curve. Mostly it's a game of trade-offs, balancing risks and rewards, and things happening at cross-purposes. Here's one example.

Yesterday I was running a medium grade fever from a suspected infection. That meant they couldn't do a needed blood transfusion because they need my temperature to be normal. If any fever then appears, they infer it is from the new blood and take appropriate measures. At the same time, my fever wasn't high enough to productively draw blood for a blood culture to identify the infection; that's best done when the fever spikes and the infection is most readily identified. So, they were simultaneously waiting for my fever to be either higher or lower to take the appropriate action.

They eventually did the blood transfusion at 9 PM last night when my fever leveled out. When it spiked again at 4 AM, they moved in like vampires, with a person from the lab drawing blood with a needle stick from my left arm while my regular nurse simultaneously drew blood from my Hickman port, a surgically implanted device in my chest that provides a two-way street so they can import IV antibiotics or export my own blood when needed. Given the volume of blood they take out, it's no wonder I need the occasional infusion just to keep supplying the damn blood draws.

On a positive note, my white blood cells have finally begun to move significantly in the hoped-for direction, meaning my body is now producing its own neutrophils (crucial to fighting infection) after the chemo-induced devastation that had eliminated virtually all such cells.

On a more suspenseful note, they did another bone marrow biopsy yesterday. I should have results later today or tomorrow. If no cancer was found, we can begin looking toward a discharge date, assuming my white blood cell count continues to improve. If cancer is still there, it's back to square one with more chemo and recovery time.

Meanwhile, Sue has received a discharge date from her transitional care unit; she will leave next Thursday, July 21. In theory, they don't release people unless they are cleared by physical and occupational therapy to be able to function in their own home. In reality, Sue has ongoing concerns about navigating our house and its two stories in my presumed absence. At this point, it's a bit unclear and more than a bit unnerving that we don't know how this will play out. Among the options is Sue moving in with her sister, renting a one-level apartment, living on one level of our house, recruiting relatives, friends, or neighbors to look in on her, or who knows what else. Hopefully, the next week will bring some needed clarity.

One productive thing that happened today was a home visit with Sue, her sister, and her physical therapist. This way the physical therapist can see our home and the challenges it presents to Sue and see how well she can navigate our stairs, hallways, and the rest. She said by phone that she was able to walk up the stairs unassisted but under close observation. With another week of physical therapy at the transitional care unit, she may feel more confident about returning home.

Finally, we await the resolution of our insurance claim for the downed trees, damaged roofs and deck, and the rest of the carnage that occurred in the wake of last week's storm. If nothing else, that little adventure has kept me from brooding on my health issues. After all, who doesn't like spending hours on the phone from a hospital bed with tree removal services, insurance adjustors, contractors, and roofers?

I also learned from Sue's phone call today that we have some internal water damage on the ceiling of the family room. This is the first time anyone has been able to assess internal damage, so now we need to get the insurance adjuster back to the house at a time when Sue's sister can meet him and let him in the house to assess the internal damage. I get it that life isn't fair, but it would be nice to catch a break after the last month of unhappy developments (sorry for whining).

As always, we conclude with the joke.

Joke of the Day:
An agnostic, dyslexic insomniac walks into a bar.

The bartender serves him a drink and says, "Hey pal, you look really tired."

The guy says, "Tell me about it. I lay awake every night wondering if there really is a Dog."

Cheers,
Steve

News Flash: Steve Whines and Catches a Break
July 14, 2016

Hi All,

You may recall my uncharacteristic whine about not catching a break in my last missive. Apparently, the squeaky wheel gets the grease, as I was just informed that my bone marrow biopsy from yesterday came back cancer free (for now, by this method). If my white blood cell count continues to improve and I remain fever-free, I may go home as early as Monday. Had they found cancer remaining, I would be looking at another month here with no break.

This will complete the "induction" phase of treatment, to be followed by the "consolidation" phase, which could have me back here in a few weeks for alternating weeks of inpatient chemo and time at home. But we'll take the good news for now where we can find it.

I'll share credit with all of you who sent emails, thoughts, prayers, and get-well cards; it helped my spirits and that can't have been bad for the outcome.

The joke department is closed for the day but will be

back on the job soon. In any case, this notice is no joke.

Cheers,
Steve

Holding Steady
July 16, 2016

Hi All,

Some of you may recall that Sue made a quick visit home last Thursday with the assistance of her sister. They discovered water stains on the family room ceiling. On Saturday, Sue's sister (who has been nominated to sainthood for her unfailing assistance to us through this adventure) returned to our house with the insurance adjustor, who has confirmed that the internal damage is due to the puncture in the roof over the family room that allowed water to enter before our neighbor temporarily plugged the hole to prevent further damage.

The inspector was on the verge of turning in our claim, which he will now revise to recommend insurance coverage for new insulation (which got wet) and a stain-concealing paint to repaint the ceiling. The drywall itself which comprises the ceiling is okay, which greatly simplifies the internal repairs since the contractor won't have to tear out and replace the ceiling. Thanks again to our good neighbor for plugging the hole in the roof and preventing further water damage.

On the medical front, not much is new. I currently have

no infections or noteworthy fevers. I am just waiting for my white blood cell count, my absolute neutrophil count (ANC), and my overall immunity to recover a bit more. Until I got here, I thought ANC referred to the African National Congress, which helped overthrow apartheid in South Africa. Given that history, I figure if I get more ANC fighters on my side, I'll have the upper hand against bacteria, viruses, fungi, and other bad guys. Best guess is that my discharge will happen next Tuesday, but it's a fluid situation.

Today is day 31 in the hospital, and I thought I deserved a little diversion. I tried to log on to a free, online poker site that I occasionally patronize from home (you "gamble" with play money on this site). It turns out that it is the only website I have tried to access so far that is blocked by my insurer who controls the Wi-Fi service in the hospital. Score one for paternalism and the power of "we know what's best for you." I can't even imagine how many cancer patients have developed incurable gambling addictions by playing free poker from their bedside while recovering from chemotherapy.

In such a world, we need a joke.

Joke of the Day (compliments of Bryan, one of my oncology consultants):

A guy walks into a bar, orders a drink, and sits down at the bar. After a while, someone in the bar shouts "47" and everybody laughs. A few minutes later, someone else yells "29" and again the bar explodes with laughter. Finally, the guy asks the bartender why everyone is laughing.

The bartender explains that everyone in there is a regular and they all know the jokes by heart. They "tell" the joke just by referencing the number and everybody knows the punchline and laughs in response. After another drink, the guy is emboldened enough to yell out "13" but the bar remains completely silent.

The guy asks the bartender what's up.

The bartender shakes his head and says, "Well, some people just don't know how to tell a joke."

Cheers,
Steve

Groundhog Days
July 18, 2016

Hi All,

I seem to be living in the world of Bill Murray's *Groundhog Day*. Every day seems like a repeat of the previous day, only with slowly rising white blood cell and neutrophil counts that will eventually reach a level that allows me to go home. Best guess is Wednesday or Thursday, but it's all about the counts.

While my white blood cells are lagging, my platelets are well within the normal range. Thus, it only seems logical to me to offer to trade platelets with some patient who has a surplus of white blood cells. For some reason, the otherwise helpful nursing staff doesn't seem to take me seriously when I make this offer, so go figure.

The big excitement around here is that they have opened up the newly-remodeled fifth floor oncology wing. I snuck up there the other day to investigate and found expansive rooms with sleeper/sofas for guests, faux fireplaces in the lounges, lots of wood, and the complete absence of bad smells. They offered to move me up there, but after thirty-three days in 4 East 3 and only a couple more to go, it didn't seem worth the effort. I'll probably land up there when I come back for consolidation chemo in a couple of weeks.

Sue will be released unconditionally from her transitional care unit on Thursday. I participated in a conference call with her discharge team today, and they are lining up in-house physical therapy, occupational therapy, home nurse visits for medical monitoring, and home aide visits for assistance with showering and perhaps some meal preparation. It's a good support system, and allegedly, all covered by insurance. I think that support and her progress at navigating the stairs at her TCU have put her (and my) mind at ease about her transition.

Meanwhile, we await the initial insurance payment for our storm damage, a total covering only the depreciated value of the damage to our house, minus our deductible. Once we hire people to actually do the work, they will provide further funds to cover full replacement value. We first have to demonstrate that we didn't take their initial check and run off to Vegas to try and double our money, which is kind of a tempting prospect, except I know full well that the house odds would be against us and that basic strategies of bankroll management speak against such frivolity, except in the movies.

Enough trivia; let's move on to the joke.

Joke of the Day (compliments of my colleague, Bill):

A guy and his dog walk into a bar. The guy says his dog can talk and he will prove it, if the bartender gives him a free drink.

The bartender plays along.

The guy asks his dog, "What keeps rain out of a house?"

The dog says "Rrrrrroof, rrrrrroof."

The bartender says, "Get out of here," but the guy insists the dog can really talk and knows a lot about sports.

The bartender relents, and the guy instructs his dog to tell people where you end up if you miss the fairway while golfing.

The dog perks up and says, "Rrrrrrrruff, rrrrrrufff."

The bartender is irate, but the crowd is intrigued as the

guy pleads for one more chance to prove his dog can talk. He asks the dog to identify the greatest player in the history of baseball.

The dog gets a twinkle in his eye and proudly responds, "Rrrrrrruth, rrrrrrruth."

Pushed over the edge, the bartender grabs the guy and his dog and throws them out the door into the street. As they amble off, the dog looks over at the guy and says "DiMaggio?"

Cheers,
Steve

Drama Queen
July 20, 2016

Hi All,

So, the long-awaited report on the genetic composition of my specific cancer is finally in. It only took 6 weeks from the initial biopsy that provided both my diagnosis and the tissue sample for the genetic testing to get these results. This is the report that promised to clearly discriminate between two alternative long-term treatments. The first option would be more chemo as an inpatient on alternating weeks in response to a milder cancer. The second option would be a stem cell transplant as a more intensive treatment in response to a more virulent cancer.

To simplify a 5-page report of highly technical gobbledygook, there are three critical indicators. The first was negative, but that's a good thing and points toward the simpler chemo route. The second was negative, but that's a bad thing and it points toward the intensive transplant route. The third indicator—the tie-breaker if you will—(insert dramatic drumroll here) was inconclusive, because they did not have a sufficient sample to make an interpretation and break the tie. Hence, my new title of drama queen.

So, short-term, I'm still hoping to get home for at least a week once my white blood cell count and absolute neutrophil count inch just a bit higher.

Long-term, I will go to the University of Minnesota Medical Center to talk to the stem cell experts in a couple of weeks. Regular hospitals do not do transplants, so the U. of M. folks are in the best position to fully interpret my ambiguous test results, discuss risks and rewards of both courses of action, and help me make an informed decision about long-term treatment.

Fortunately, Sue is still scheduled to return home tomorrow. For those of you who bet on Sue to return home first, you may collect your winnings at window A. After thirty-four days of a completely empty nest, it will be good to have at least one person living at home to water whichever plants have survived, turn lights on and off, and the rest. I'm sure our local support team will also appreciate the opportunity to stand down. Our thanks again to those team members.

Whew! Enough for one day. I hope you enjoyed the talking dog joke from my last email; today we continue the dog theme as we present the joke.

Joke of the Day:
Trigger Warning: Easy, people. It's just a joke. I can assure you that no real dogs were harmed in the writing of this joke.

A blind man and his service dog walk into a bar. They proceed to the middle of the room, where the man picks up the dog by the tail and swings the dog over his head in a wide arc.

The bartender rushes up and says, "Hold on there, buddy; what are you doing?"

The blind guy answers, "Just having a look around."

Cheers,
Steve

Countdown to Launch
July 21, 2016

Hi All,

My absolute neutrophil count has finally reached the magic number of 1.0, meaning I now have enough white blood cells and restored immunity to venture out into the big, germ-filled world once again. In addition, I have been taken off all IV fluids, antibiotics, antivirals, anti-fungals, and whatever other anti-s they have had me on.

Assuming my count stays at 1.0 or better and I have no new fevers or infections in the next 20+ hours, I should be discharged tomorrow around the noon hour. Long term treatment has yet to be determined, but I'm hoping for at least a week at home and a semblance of normality during that time.

Even as I write this, Sue is arriving at home, having been discharged from her TCU today. Now life's about really mundane stuff like restocking groceries, preparing meals, catching up on mail, and—oh yeah—finding people to repair our storm damage.

On that short and sweet note, we have an equally succinct joke.

Joke of the Day:
A skeleton walks into a bar and says to the bartender, "Give me a beer…and a mop."

Cheers,
Steve

2. At Home: A Welcome Respite (Can I Have My Life Back Now?)

"The ill person needs to reaffirm that his story is worth listening to by others. He must also reaffirm that he is still there, as an audience for himself."
—Arthur Frank, from *The Wounded Storyteller*

The following reports were composed from late July to late August of 2016 and sent to a widening circle of acquaintances and colleagues. It was a sweet interlude at a wonderful time of year. I had weathered my initial treatment reasonably well and was feeling pretty good. Sue was home, and I was able to resume many of my normal activities. Looming over all of it, however, was the need to reach a decision about the next step and the knowledge that I would be undergoing an even more consequential round of treatment in the coming weeks and months ahead. I relished every minute of my "normal" life while also planning for what would come next.

Home
July 23, 2016

Hi All,

As you may recall, on Thursday my absolute neutrophil count reached 1.0, the magic number needed for hospital discharge on Friday. Apparently needing a bit more drama, however, my Friday morning ANC dropped back to .9, jeopardizing my discharge.

After a couple of hours in limbo (half-packed, wondering whether to finish packing for home or unpack for a longer hospital stay), my oncologist gave me the green light to go home as scheduled, despite the dip in the number. Just to be cautious, I will return on Monday as an outpatient for a blood draw to verify that the .9 was a temporary blip and not a downward trend.

It seemed only fitting that my long-time friend, colleague, and commuting partner provided my ride home. For most of my academic career, Tom and I shared the three-hour round-trip commute from home to campus two to three times per week, thirty-two weeks per year, twenty years running, rain, shine, and some memorable blizzards. That's a lot of trips, but none were sweeter than yesterday's short hop from hospital to home.

If you were to watch a video of Sue and me navigating

our house, you would swear that video was running in slow motion. Between her recovery from surgery, chronic fibromyalgia, and psoriatic arthritis and my post-chemo fatigue, things are moving very slow for us right now. On the other hand, things that once seemed urgent appear quite trivial now. In any event, we're getting lots of practice at prioritizing activities, focusing on the task at hand, and getting plenty of R and R.

For now, I will remain home, as long as no fevers or infections occur. I have weekly outpatient appointments every Friday through August for blood draws and monitoring. On August 4, I am tentatively scheduled for a 3-hour consultation at the U. of M. to discuss additional treatment—either more chemo or a stem cell transplant. The following week I will meet with my oncologist to put all the pieces together and reach a decision.

For the time being, I am happy to be home, optimistic about the future, and grateful for your support. The joke department is temporarily closed for inventory and restocking, but will be open for business again as the need arises.

Peace,
Steve

Fun with Numbers
July 26, 2016

Hi All,

I have had no fevers or infections since leaving the hospital on Friday, but I did return to the hospital as an outpatient on Monday for a blood draw. The results were rather intriguing.

During my inpatient stay, it took my white blood cell count twelve days to recover from a chemo-induced low point of .2 up to 1.7. Upon leaving the hospital, it took a mere three days to go from 1.7 to 4.1 (normal range for healthy folks = 3.8-11.0).

It took over two weeks to have a neutrophil count that registered during my inpatient stay, and then another nine days to go from .2 to .9. Upon leaving the hospital, it took a mere three days to go from .9 to 3.1 (normal range for healthy folks = 2.0-6.8).

Apparently, hospitals are bad for my health and home is good. Not only are these results in the normal range, they are better than I have registered for a couple years (well before the leukemia diagnosis).

The increase was so dramatic that my nurse worried that I might have an as-yet undetected viral infection that was pushing my immune system into overdrive and that would not be a good thing.

With further checking, it turns out that before I left the hospital, a nurse gave me an injection of a drug meant to spur my own bone marrow to begin producing white blood cells and neutrophils.

They must have slipped this one by me, because I was not aware that I received this treatment. After dozens of blood draws, several transfusions of red blood cells and platelets, almost two dozen antibiotics, several anti-viral and anti-fungal medications, and countless measurements of vital signs, I can't imagine how I missed this. It seems, however, it might have been a good idea to give me this drug even earlier, but what do I know?

In any event, my response to this drug is exactly what they hoped for; in fact, it's at the upper end of what could be expected. I have no idea if this "recovery" is a long-term result or a temporary blip, nor do I know if it has any implications for the follow-up treatment still to be determined.

What I do know is that my follow-up treatment down the road (chemo or transplant) will involve destroying all these wonderful white blood cells and neutrophils all over again, only to build them back up again. That seems rather sad, but it's the price to be paid for minimizing the chance that the cancer will return.

Meanwhile, on the home front, we have roofers coming today and tomorrow for estimates on repairs. Sue has an occupational therapist coming this morning and a physical therapist visiting this afternoon. My afternoon adventures will take me to the grocery store for some much-needed restocking, and the rest of the week will bring his and hers follow-up medical appointments.

So, we're busy, but I *am* enjoying this little hiatus, and the opportunity to build my mental, physical, and emotional reserves for whatever comes next.

The joke department inventory is proceeding, but they did discover a pharmacy joke misfiled among the bar jokes, so here goes.

Joke of the Day:
A duck walks into a pharmacy and says, "Give me some chapstick; put it on my bill."

Cheers,
Steve

The Eyes Have It
August 2, 2016

Hi All,

After thirty-seven days of captivity, I am loving my time at home and doing normal things like going for my annual eye exam with my optometrist. As you probably know, this is the person that changes your eyeglass prescription just enough every year that you feel compelled to buy new glasses.

Toward the end of yesterday's exam, he asked if I wouldn't mind waiting while he looked something up in a book. In an era of internet-driven information, I found this request rather charming. He came back and said he thought I should see an ophthalmologist, and that they just happened to have one in the clinic, if I could wait an hour and a half.

After amusing myself in every conceivable way, I was reduced to skimming through a magazine completely dedicated to celebrity claptrap, a cultural artifact that I do not think speaks well for the human condition.

So, the ophthalmologist found areas of swelling in the tiny capillaries of my retinas that are probably due to the leukemia and will resolve if/when the cancer goes into full remission. I have no visual impairment now, so they will simply monitor it with some really cool baseline pictures of my retinas that they took. As an added precaution, they are sending me to see another ophthalmologist who is a retinal specialist, just to make sure this problem will not be exacerbated with additional chemotherapy treatments.

So much for doing normal stuff again!

Meanwhile, I have a three-hour appointment at the U of M blood and marrow transplant department on Thursday the 4th to discuss my options for future treatment. The following Friday (the 12th), I will meet with my oncologist to make the big decision.

Given that the least disruptive treatment would involve alternating weeks of in-patient IV chemotherapy and weeks at home well into September, I have concluded that I will not be able to teach this fall semester. Hence, I am filing the paperwork to activate my accumulated sick leave and long-term disability coverage at least through the fall semester. I am grateful there is no financial pressure on me to teach, although I'd rather be able to do so.

Meanwhile, in another part of our life, our storm-related damage will soon get some needed attention. We are scheduled to get a new roof and gutters early next week. Deck repairs will follow, and the last chapter of the story will involve replacing the insulation above the garage and family room and repainting the family room ceiling where the house took on some water.

Last week, our contractor met face-to-face with the insurance adjustor to discuss why some things were covered and others were not, and how the dollar figures were calculated. Both these guys are twenty plus year veterans in their respective roles and it was like watching two prize fighters or chess players making their best moves.

The contractor made an eloquent case for why we should get more insurance coverage (most of which would go to him) while the insurance adjustor defended his estimates and sought to minimize the insurance payout. There was a little give and take on both sides, but I think we will be able to break even on the money and simply "pay" for the new roof with the hassle and inconvenience required to get it done.

Finally, after some insurance snafus, Sue is once again receiving home care in the form of nurse visits, physical therapy, and occupational therapy; she is also considering a home health aide to assist with various chores. This will become more important when I return to the hospital for further treatment, but she is getting stronger, moving better, and gradually returning to some of her routine activities.

The joke department is once again open, so here goes.

Joke of the Day:

An Ivy League college graduate walks into a bar frequented by big, burly Texans. One regular patron says, "Howdy stranger, where are you from?"

The graduate says, "I come from a place where we do not end our sentences in prepositions."

The Texan replies, "Oh, I'm sorry. Where are you from, *jackass*?"

Cheers,
Steve

Got Advice?
August 5, 2016

Hi All,

I hope these emails have been helpful in keeping people updated about our status. For my part, composing them has been therapeutic because it requires me to create a coherent narrative out of some seemingly random and chaotic events. Today, I hope to accomplish a third goal as well.

The thirty-plus people receiving these emails collectively know many more people, and some of them have doubtless gone through something like what I am facing. So, if you or they have advice, cautions, or recommendations on my next steps, I welcome anything you can offer by email or phone (especially on caregivers discussed at the end of this note).

First, an update. Yesterday I met with the transplant folks at the U of M to discuss the next stage of treatment. One option is multiple rounds of high dose chemotherapy. The five-year survival rate for this option is 33%. More-over, people over sixty (I'm sixty-four) sometimes cannot tolerate this regimen and must terminate treatment before realizing the benefits, or run the risk of coma or organ failure due to the chemo. My new oncologist does not recommend this option and would refer me to someone else if I wanted to pursue it.

The other option is a reduced intensity (due to my age) stem cell transplant. There is a 15-20% mortality rate from the transplant itself. After that, the survival rate approximates 50% five years out with the chance of a much longer remission. This treatment and initial recovery runs for approximately one hundred days (really).

For the first five weeks, I would be an inpatient as they administer chemo and radiation to obliterate my bone marrow, perform the transplant, and monitor me for infections, including graft versus host disease. In this scenario, my body would initially attack the transplanted stem cells and then as they engraft, they would attack my unfamiliar body as a foreign threat to them.

For the next ten weeks, I would be an outpatient living at home. For the first four weeks of this period, I would need to make daily visits to the clinic for follow-up care and treatment. For the next six weeks, these visits would taper down to 2 or 3 visits per week. This is the treatment my new oncologist at the U of M recommends, which echoes the advice of my previous oncologist during my stay at Methodist Hospital.

The ten weeks as an outpatient require that I have a caregiver on hand around the clock (i. e., living in my house). They would perform mundane tasks that might be beyond my capacity, drive me to the clinic visits, and get me to the hospital on short notice if I have a serious complication or relapse. While this role is important, it can be shared; one patient recruited no fewer than 37 caregivers to play the role for two or three days at a time.

This seems a bit extreme to me, but the oncologist is quite serious about the potential complications and need for continuous and timely support. Our hope is that Sue can fulfill some of these duties, but given her own health issues this isn't a guarantee. She is also not able to provide cross-town transportation, on a daily basis or on short notice.

We will have to get creative to pull this off. If you know how other people have addressed this challenge, I especially welcome your input. Beyond relatives (few and far between) and close friends, it has been suggested that I contact nursing programs for aspiring students or retired nurses who could be a caregiver for a limited time and a mutually agreeable fee. I'm open to any suggestions you may have (the social worker at the hospital recommended that I do not recruit a caregiver through online want ads. Duh!).

In the meantime, I do plan to get a second (or third, counting both my oncologists) opinion from the Mayo Clinic in the next week or two, but I'm guessing the transplant route will be the direction I will go.

All this planning makes my current time at home (fourteen "healthy" days and counting) sweeter than ever, but I should probably begin the next phase of treatment within a month or less before the cancer has a chance to return and complicate the follow-up treatment.

In my mind, the somber tone of this missive makes the joke of the day more important. I have no idea why this joke is set in Paris, but it comes from my good friend, Dave.

Joke of the Day:
A guy walks into a bar in Paris with a duck on his head (coincidentally, the duck has chapstick on his bill from a previous joke).

The bartender looks at the duo and says, "Well, that is really unusual. Where did you find him?"

The duck says, "It was easy; there's hundreds of them walking around out there."

Cheers,
Steve

Decisions, Decisions
August 20, 2016

Hi All,

After thirty-seven days in the hospital, I've logged twenty-nine days on probation at home. In that time, I've had no fevers or infections (other than a three-four day common cold) and my only cancer/chemo-related symptom has been some fatigue that responds well to afternoon naps. Moreover, all my counts (hemoglobin, white blood cells, platelets, and neutrophils) are back in the normal range and better than they have been in years.

It's a tempting fantasy to think I'm "cured," but all the medical evidence suggests that this cancer will come roaring back within weeks. Even though the "induction" phase was highly successful, a "consolidation" phase is mandatory. They want to start that phase when I am cancer-free, so if we don't get to it within a few weeks, they may have to give me another dose of chemo to bridge to the consolidation phase. Hence, my days on probation are numbered.

In my last email, I summarized the recommendation from the U of M oncologist that I have a stem cell transplant. Since then, we have learned that my brother and potential donor, Jerome, is a half-match, which is not as good as a full match but much better than a half-wit. Half-match is the most common relation between siblings, and essentially means we got the same stuff from one parent but different stuff from the other. Transplants can be done with half-matches, but there is some risk of rejection because of the non-matching half.

Hence, the U of M is now searching national blood banks for umbilical cord blood that might provide a closer match and lower chance of rejection. With a good match, this would be the way to go since these cells have no significant "memory" of another body and are less likely to mistakenly attack my body. The downside may be finding enough cells to do the job and waiting for them to engraft and grow new cells once the transplant is done.

If I pursue the stem cell route, those are the issues and decisions yet to be resolved. In the bigger picture, I still have the option of avoiding the transplant and doing several rounds of high-dose chemotherapy instead.

The oncologist at the U of M recommended against this route because older folks often don't tolerate the treatment well and even if they do, the five-year survival rate is not great. I have since been to the Mayo clinic for a second opinion; in a nutshell, the oncologist there independently favored the transplant over chemo for the same reasons.

Sue and I met yesterday with my oncologist from my earlier Methodist Hospital stay to process all this information. We reviewed the data that places me in an "intermediate" risk category, as well as the benefits and risks of both treatment options. When pushed for an opinion, this oncologist also said she "leaned" toward the transplant even while she was reiterating the dangers.

Sue then asked the classic question of what my oncologist would recommend if it was her husband needing treatment, and she said without hesitation that she would favor the transplant. (Of course, the premise behind this question is that the marriage in question is a happy one and that the respondent wants the spouse to survive, but it's probably best not to overthink this one.)

So, all that points toward a transplant. The closer the cord blood match they find, the easier that final decision will be. The Methodist Hospital oncologist will call the U of M early next week to see where things stand, so I should know more soon.

I've been advised to gather as much information as possible about all this and then go with my gut instinct for the final decision. Right now, my gut says if I go the chemo route and it doesn't work out, I will kick myself around the block for not trying the transplant route. If I go the transplant route and it doesn't work, I will feel like I gave it my best shot and it just wasn't meant to be. We'll see what my gut says next week.

If I do the transplant, I will need caregivers when I return home after roughly 5 weeks as an inpatient. My thanks to everyone who offered caregiver suggestions in response to my last email, and my heartfelt thanks to those of you who volunteered to help in whatever capacity you can. With your responses, I'm feeling more confident that we can pull it off.

Meanwhile, life goes on. Sue continues to impress her physical therapist with her progress and has begun to drive again, so she is regaining a degree of independence. She will also be seeing a rheumatologist to transition away from her long-term use of prednisone toward a biologic medication to help control her chronic pain from psoriatic arthritis and fibromyalgia.

This change is overdue, as the side-effects from the prednisone have eclipsed the benefits and she needs another method to control her symptoms. She will also be exploring the option of medical marijuana, as Minnesota recently approved its use for intractable pain and she should qualify by this standard.

As of August 9, we have a new roof. It was a potentially rainy installation day, so they sent a double crew who started and completed the entire job in little over five hours. The new shingles have some subtle coloring that picks up the sage green exterior paint on our house. Neighbors driving by have given the thumbs up, so that's what really counts.

With apologies for perhaps writing more than you needed or wanted to know, we return to the tradition of the joke.

Joke of the Day:

A panda walks into a bar and gobbles some beer nuts. Then he pulls out a gun, fires it in the air, and heads for the door.

"Hey!" shouts the bartender.

The panda yells back, "I'm a panda. Google me!"

Sure enough: Panda: "A tree-climbing mammal with distinct black-and-white coloring. Eats shoots and leaves."

Cheers,
Steve

Decisions Are a Process
August 27, 2016

Hi All,

I'm probably incapable of providing a *brief* update, but I'll try.

Since my last email, I made a second trip to the Mayo clinic (compliments of my chauffeur, colleague, and co-conspirator, Tom) to get additional opinions from two transplant specialists. Some three hours later, we left very impressed with the consultation. (The bill is equally impressive.)

They concurred with the advice I've received to date, while adding some details and nuance. Most importantly, they also recommend I have a transplant over chemotherapy, given my relatively good health and assuming a suitable donor. While Mayo is not a feasible option for the procedure itself because of its distance from home, their perspective was reassuring.

On the ride home, I received a call from the U of M transplant center that they have umbilical cord blood matches for me, in addition to my brother who is a half-match donor.

There is no way to know which option is better because both sources have virtually identical five-year survival rates. They invited me to participate in a study where I would be randomly assigned to either my brother or the cord blood for the stem cells.

The trade-off looks like this. With a half-match relative, there is a slightly lower risk of infection and smoother engraftment but a slightly higher relapse rate. With cord blood, there is a slightly higher rate of infection and more prolonged period of engraftment, but a slightly lower relapse rate. Five years out, it all balances out to equal survival rates.

If I decline the study, the people at the U of M recommend using the cord blood because that's their specialty. If I enter the study, I have a 50-50 chance of drawing my brother or the cord blood. Having read the 22-page consent form for the study, I have numerous questions to ask before agreeing to it or opting out, but still receiving a transplant, presumably from the cord blood sample.

Meanwhile, I have not had any chemotherapy since June 23 and because this cancer comes back so rapidly, there is a consensus that I should have one round of consolidation chemo to keep the disease in remission while we take the final steps to set the transplant in motion.

My fall calendar now looks something like this. I will spend the week of August 29 at Methodist Hospital receiving chemo. I will then spend approximately three weeks at home while my counts recover sufficiently to have the transplant at the U of M, but this could take longer. Allowing for a week of work-up testing, the transplant could occur at the end of September or beginning of October.

I would then spend four to five weeks as an inpatient, followed by ten weeks of follow-up treatment as an outpatient (this is the time when the caregivers will be needed). That takes me to the end of a year I'll be happy to leave behind.

Meanwhile, our house recovery has stalled a bit as we wait on gutters and deck repairs. Sue, however, has not stalled but rather continues to gain strength and mobility. She had her last session with her physical therapist this week and can be seen around the house striking odd poses and going through strange motions that she assures me are part of her rehabilitation program.

So much for trying to be *brief*. Let me compensate with a very concise joke; pay attention or it will get past you before you know it.

Joke of the Day:
A guy walks into a bar and is knocked unconscious for three days.

Cheers,
Steve

3. The Hospital to Home Merry-Go-Round (Stop the Ride, I Want to Get Off)

"Turning illness into story is a kind of meta-control..."
—Arthur Frank, from *The Wounded Storyteller*

The following reports were composed from late August to early October of 2016. This period started with a planned, week-long hospital stay for "consolidation chemotherapy" to keep my leukemia in remission until I could begin the transplant process. It also included an unplanned, emergency return to the hospital for several days in response to side-effects from the chemotherapy. It concluded with preparations for my admission to the University of Minnesota Medical Center for the transplant.

Quick Update
August 29, 2016

Hey Folks,

Just a quick note on my new digs. I'm on the refurbished 5th floor cancer/chemo ward at Methodist Hospital. Spacious room, nice wood accents, sleeper/sofa for a guest, and it smells pleasant because it's all new, fresh and clean.

I've been roaming the halls and reconnecting with several of my favorite nurses and my very atypical chaplain. If I must be in a hospital right now (and they tell me that I do), this is the place I want to be.

My regimen is to receive high-dose chemotherapy through a three-hour infusion twice a day at twelve-hour intervals on Monday, Wednesday, and Friday and go home on Saturday. The first dose is pending any time today, once they get the routine lab results. I'm optimistic that the pre-meds will control the immediate side-effects, and other medications will lessen the chances of infection once I return home.

I'll be in touch as developments warrant.

Cheers,
Steve

Smooth Sailing
September 1, 2016

Hi All,

My last update was a couple of days ago, but I have been verbally excoriated by a former graduate student (who shall remain anonymous) for not including a joke of the day with that email. I take this as evidence of how well we train our graduate students to be astute observers of their social world and to not be bashful about reporting their observations.

So, as a conscientious professor responding to the quasi-legitimate concerns of a terrific former student and current friend, I offer this report (with joke). Last night I received my fourth infusion of high dose chemotherapy. So far, I am passing all the neurological tests before each infusion (meaning my brain has not been fried yet), and with the pre-meds I have no nausea or other gastrointestinal indignities.

Indeed, the oddest symptom was Tuesday when I came down with…don't laugh…a case of hiccups that wouldn't quit. (Okay, fess up; I know you laughed a little bit at the hiccups part because they're somehow inherently funny if they're not happening to you—yes?)

I self-diagnosed it to the steroids they use in the pre-meds before chemo and tried about a dozen goofy home remedies for hiccups off the web before I found one that worked like a charm.

Looking ahead, the short-term plan is for two more doses of chemo on Friday and a discharge home on Saturday. They will send me out the door with a dose of a drug that should help restore the white blood cells and neutrophils they are currently killing off. Hopefully, it will shorten the period of immunosuppression and vulnerability to any infection that crosses my path.

The long-term plan will involve the stem cell transplant at the U of M once I clear a few more hurdles. First, my white blood cell count and neutrophils must return to an acceptable level. Second, a bone marrow biopsy (my fifth) must be done to confirm that I am still in remission. Third, I must go through a week of "work-up" to determine that my heart, lungs, and other vital organs are able to withstand the challenges of the transplant.

That will put me on their rough calendar as previously outlined.

More details as they become available, but now we return to tradition with the joke.

Joke of the Day:
An affluent patron was about to walk into a bar when he noticed a down-and-out older man fishing in a tiny pond outside the bar. He took pity on the guy and invited him in for a drink.

As they sipped their whiskeys, the benefactor thought he'd humor the old man and asked, "So how many have you caught today?"

The old man replied, "You're the eighth."

Cheers,
Steve

Really Quick Update
September 1, 2016

Hi All,

Okay, now I'm getting heat from my department chair for not sharing the hiccups remedy since "everybody" wants to know. I'll share it here.

The remedy is even funnier than the hiccups. I pieced it together from a couple suggestions on the web. If you have an assistant, they could help you if they don't laugh too hard, but as a solo act you can do this.

Fill a cup of water and place a straw in it.

Then place one thumb in each ear, reach across the front of your face and pinch both nostrils with your little fingers.

Take two or three sips on the straw and hold your breath (mouth on straw, straw in water) as long as you can.

I guess the idea is that you want nothing going in or out of any orifice above your neck, and that somehow tells your diaphragm to relax. Viola! Hiccups gone.

I'm smiling as I picture all of you rehearsing this.

Cheers,
Steve

Holding Pattern
September 4, 2016

Hi All,

As expected, I was discharged from the hospital on Saturday morning after some follow-up chemo treatments to keep my cancer in remission until I can begin the stem cell procedure in early October. Other than the infamous and highly popular hiccups episode, I had no problems with the chemo or my hospital staycation.

After induction chemo, they kept me in the hospital for four weeks to monitor infections in the wake of immunosuppression. After chemo this Friday, they sent me out the door the next day with medications to prevent or mitigate infections. They also gave me strict guidelines about when to call or come in if something nasty starts.

This next week is expected to be relatively smooth, but I expect my counts will bottom out the week of the 11th. That's when the real effects of the chemo just completed will announce themselves, and when I'll be at the greatest risk for infection and will take extra precautions.

Meanwhile, I will return to the clinic three days a week for blood draws and assessments, so between my monitoring and their oversight we should catch anything that happens in a timely manner. Once the counts come up, I should be ready to embark on the transplant.

The journey so far has been thirty-seven days in the hospital for induction chemo, followed by a (coincidentally equal) thirty-seven days at home for recovery, then five days in the hospital for consolidation chemo, and hopefully another clean month at home before I hit the backstretch of this race with the transplant.

Many clichés fit here: one day at a time, you can't rush it, take it as it comes, or whatever. I remain pleased with my mindfulness practice, meditation and yoga. They help me to accept and live within whatever parameters the world puts around me for now. This experience has a way of clarifying priorities like nothing else I've been through. I'm learning there are trade-offs to be found out of something that no one *should* have to go through, but so it goes.

As I notice little side effects and medication challenges, it's evident I will need some help from Sue as well as the other way around. She seems equal to the challenge. We're finding our way to a more balanced relationship; now we *both* sit at the kitchen table in the morning trying to sort through which of our respective medications to take before, with, or after meals, in varying doses, at non-synchronized times, etc. To paraphrase an old saying, I guess the family that medicates together stays together.

Unless something noteworthy happens, I'll probably slow the pace of these email communications and let you go about your business. Every email, phone call, or card I have received has meant a lot to me during this period and I will continue to appreciate whatever support people are able to offer. And now, the joke.

Joke of the Day:
A duck (with chapstick on his bill from a previous joke) walks into a bar, and asks the bartender, "Do you have any grapes?"

The bartender says, "No, we only sell beer here."

So, the duck leaves.

The next day, the duck returns and asks the bartender, "Do you have any grapes?"

The bartender says, "No, I told you we only sell beer, and if you ask me again I'm going to nail your bill to the bar."

So, the duck leaves.

The next day the duck walks back into the bar, and asks the bartender, "Do you have any nails?"

The bartender says, "No."

So, the duck asks, "Do you have any grapes?"

Peace,
Steve

Oops!
September 10, 2016

Hi All,

Have you ever awakened in the middle of the night with symptoms that might require a trip to urgent care or the emergency room and you had to decide how to proceed? Me, too.

At 3 AM Saturday morning, I noticed a low-grade fever that persisted for the next six hours. That was okay, but I also had unusual bleeding (I'll spare you the details) which is a trigger for me to call the nurse line.

Two calls, some more sleep, and seven hours later with symptoms persisting, they called me into the ER. There, my white blood cell count was .3 and my platelets were 4. In the words of the ER doctor, "There's nothing there" to resist infection or promote coagulation.

At least I know they gave me top shelf chemo the week before, because it completely wiped out these otherwise handy disease fighters and clotting functions.

By 2 PM, I was getting settled into my new hospital room for platelet infusions and monitoring of my symptoms. Depending on how I respond and which doctor you believe, I could be released as early as the next day or as late as five days from now.

I requested my corner room from my last stay, but

alas, it's occupied so I'm a couple of doors away but still on the remodeled and clean-smelling fifth floor. I had a mostly-packed bag at home in anticipation of the trip, and when I whined a bit about the uncertainty, Sue played the "pregnant woman" card on me, noting that this is standard operating procedure for most women close to childbirth. Touché.

While a tad inconvenient, this is completely routine for this course of treatment. I feel bad for Sue home alone once again; at least I'm getting care, attention, and conversation with nurses, many of whom now greet me by name and know some of my patient preferences and proclivities. So here is the joke.

Joke of the Day (with an appropriate theme, compliments of my medical sociologist colleague, Catarina):

An infectious disease walks into a bar.

The bartender says, "We don't serve infectious diseases in this bar."

The infectious disease says, "Well, you are not a very good host."

Cheers,
Steve

Back on Track
September 15, 2016

Hi All,

I was discharged from the hospital yesterday morning and once again I am enjoying my time at home. Here's a brief summary of my latest hospital adventure.

I received two units of platelets on Saturday and then again on Sunday. While my overall platelet count is still low, these transfusions effectively resolved the bleeding problems I came in with. On Sunday, attention shifted to a nasty fever that spiked in the 102 F range four separate times, only to be knocked down by acetaminophen each time.

By Monday, the two broad spectrum antibiotics I was receiving began to take effect and the fever moderated that day and disappeared on Tuesday, paving the road for my discharge on Wednesday. Along the way, they did an abdominal CT scan, a chest X-ray, and multiple blood cultures. They never did identify the exact source of the infection, but the antibiotics have sent it to the Tomb of the Unknown Bacterium.

My maintenance regimen at home includes a trifecta of anti-viral, anti-fungal, and antibiotic medications to keep the bad guys at bay. Even more helpful, a shot I received on September 4 (two days after finishing chemo) has indeed stimulated the return of my white blood cells. After my counts hit bottom this time, they came back in three to four days and are now in the normal range. During my induction chemo when my body was on its own to produce white blood cells, it took three weeks to log that much progress.

As impressive as the dose has been, the price is even more so. One shot administered in less than 5 seconds was billed out just under $10,000., discounted to just under $5,000. and paid by my insurance with a $180. co-insurance payment from me. When I called the hospital billing office to make sure this was not a mistake, they sternly said this is the standard charge and acted like I was the crazy one for asking such a question.

All told, I think I'm still on schedule for my next adventure as a transplant patient. I will need to maintain my white blood cell count and have more improvement in my platelets and hemoglobin, but I'm guessing the first week of October is still the target date for the workup tests that precede the actual transplant.

Sue held the fort at home and kept several of her own medical appointments during my unexpected five-day hospitalization. For every possible reason, we're happiest when we can both be home, but this recent separation was practice and a learning experience for how she can manage during my longer hospitalization for the transplant.

Continuing the medical theme (compliments of my colleague, Catarina), I'm happy to present the joke.

Joke of the Day:
Two bacteria walk into a bar.
The bartender says, "Sorry, we don't serve bacteria in this bar."
The two bacteria say, "Hey, but we work here! We're staph."

Cheers,
Steve

Moving Forward
September 22, 2016

Hi All,

I've been home for eight days since my last hospitalization and have been enjoying my probation immensely. Several things have gone well.

Thanks to that rather expensive shot, my white blood cells and immunity have been restored more quickly than anticipated. I've completed a five-day regimen of prophylactic antibiotics with no complications. I've discontinued the prophylactic anti-viral and (eye-blurring) antifungal medications I had been taking since returning home. Last, but not least, I picked up a cool $145 over two poker sessions at our local casino and another $20 at a home tournament with a bunch of retired guys I haven't seen since my diagnosis in June.

Due to my quick recovery, I received a call earlier this week that we can begin the process leading to the stem cell transplant at the U of M a week earlier than expected. It starts with a week of work-up testing of vital organs and related bodily functions to insure I can withstand the rigors of the transplant.

The date of my eventual discharge from the hospital after the transplant will depend on how well I recover;

it will be no earlier than mid-November and could be a week or two later. Fortunately, I have an excellent support team of caregivers lined up for the first and most crucial month when I return home, so I feel about as prepared as I can be at this point. My heartfelt thanks to my colleague, Tom, and my Wisconsin team.

I've studied up on the transplant process as much as I care to. The list of probable and possible complications and side effects is quite daunting. Nothing I've read would convince a sane person that the transplant is a desirable option, except for the crucial fact that it is better than all the alternatives. After some time to process this information, I am at peace with my choice and fully committed to this course of action.

I will take with me my tool kit of mindfulness, meditation, yoga, and various forms of exercise as well as the support, prayers, healing energy, and good wishes all of you have sent my way. When combined with how well I have tolerated everything the medical staff has thrown at me, my pro-active attitude and warped sense of humor has seen me through so far. I feel about as well prepared as anyone could be going into this adventure.

In a couple of weeks, Sue will face a long stretch at home alone during my hospital stay. In anticipation of her challenges, we have instituted a "buddy of the week" program whereby various neighbors have volunteered to take a first phone call during "their" week if Sue needs assistance at home. Our thanks to those who have volunteered and filled out the first five weeks of my hospital stay with a home support system for her.

It seems appropriate to continue the medically-themed closers contributed by my colleague, Catarina, so we conclude with the joke.

Joke of the Day:
A virus walks into a bar.
The bartender says, "We don't serve viruses in this bar."

The virus replaces the bartender and says, "Now we do."

Cheers,
Steve

Full Speed Ahead
September 30, 2016

Hi All,

I've now completed my week of work-up tests and the headline is that I've been cleared for the stem cell transplant. Pending final insurance approval, I may be admitted to the hospital for pre-transplant conditioning (chemo and radiation) as soon as next Tuesday, which is almost a week earlier than initially expected.

For the curious amongst you, the work-up involved two chest X-rays, three chest CT scans, a battery of pulmonary function tests, a multi-gated acquisition scan with radionuclide tracers of my heart, an EKG of my heart, a bone marrow biopsy (showing no leukemia at present), a lumbar puncture, a urine sample, 22 vials of blood to check kidney and liver function (and who knows what else?), consultations with nurses, pharmacists, social workers, and doctors, and a partridge in a pear tree.

My personal favorite was the pulmonary function test where they had to double-check the calibration of their machinery when I exhaled 150% of the expected volume of air in my lungs. I suspect thirty-five years of lap swimming may have contributed to that outcome, but I've always been good at taking tests. When all is said and done,

Steve Buechler

my co-morbidity score is zero, meaning there is nothing in my medical past or present that they can detect that would compromise my ability to handle the transplant. So...I guess there's no turning back at this point.

During one of those blood draws, my nurse raised an intriguing possibility. Once I recover from the transplant, I could commit a crime (say, rob a bank) and leave a trace of blood at the scene. When they do DNA testing of the blood, it will lead them directly to the baby whose umbilical cord blood supplied the stem cells for my transplant. How weird is that? Of course, babies often elicit a lot of sympathy from juries, so a conviction is hardly a foregone conclusion, but it could buy me enough time to flee the country with my ill-gotten goods.

Other science fiction-like implications include the fact that if they use two different cords for my transplant, I could have three distinct DNA sequences bouncing around in my body until one cord vanquishes the other and my original DNA. Oh, and my blood type will slowly switch over from O-negative to A positive. For better or worse, however, I will retain my own fingerprints.

To celebrate this turning point, I would like to acknowledge the support of an old and dear friend. Bruna came from Italy to study in the M A sociology program at UW-Milwaukee in the mid-1970s. Along with our mutual friend, Dave, the three of us had some memorable times together. Though I haven't seen Bruna since she returned to Italy almost forty years ago, we have revived our friendship through the magic of cyberspace. Amongst our email exchanges, Bruna passed on the following joke. I'm confident you will agree that it meets the high standards for humor that have made our jokes famous (or infamous). Without further ado, we proudly present our trans-continental joke.

Joke of the Day:

A _carabinieri_ (policeman) walks into a bar and asks for a cappuccino and two croissants.

The bartender replies, "Sorry, there are no croissants

108

left this morning."

The *carabiniere* says, "It doesn't matter. I'll have a coffee with two croissants."

The bartender says, "Sorry, there are no croissants left this morning."

The *carabiniere* says, "It doesn't matter. I'll have a milkshake with two croissants."

The bartender says, "Sorry, there are no croissants left this morning."

The *carabiniere* says, "It doesn't matter. I'll have an orange juice with two croissants."

Etc., until the bartender tells the *carabiniere* to get lost.

The next day the captain of the *carabiniere* (a superior officer in the military hierarchy) walks into the same bar and the bartender tells him the story. Then he adds, "Look, I was very patient. What would you have done in my place?"

The captain says, "You were indeed! I would have thrown the two croissants into his face!"

Cheers,
Steve

The Countdown Begins
October 5, 2016

Hi All,

With my work-up completed, insurance verified, cords on the way, and Sue's endorsement, I will report to the University of Minnesota Medical Center tomorrow morning to begin the transplant process.

Now that it is imminent, let me clarify the misleadingly named "transplant" I am about to undergo. (You can take the teacher out of the classroom, but you can't keep him from teaching.)

A key player in the process is a Hickman central line that was "installed" in my chest at the beginning of this adventure in mid-June. Mr. Hickman is a handy fellow; he facilitates painless blood draws without needle sticks but also allows delivery of hydrating fluids, IV antibiotics, transfusions, chemotherapy, and…stem cells.

My so-called "transplant" is really just another "transfusion." When the time comes, a nurse will hang a bag of my donor's umbilical cord blood, hook it up to Mr. Hickman, and transfuse the cells into my bloodstream. No anesthesia, incisions, or any other surgical interventions implied by the term "transplant" will occur. It takes less than an hour. Once in my bloodstream, these stem cells gradually engraft in my bone marrow over several weeks and begin to produce healthy new blood cells.

To create a more hospitable environment, I will undergo "conditioning" starting on Friday. This involves five days of chemotherapy and one dose of total body irradiation to dampen and eventually kill off my diseased immune system and increase the chances that my body will accept the new stem cells. That sounds daunting, but due to my old age, I am receiving a "reduced intensity" conditioning regimen that will still leave some bone marrow and will not be as taxing on my body as the "full intensity" conditioning that younger folks receive.

The day after the transplant, they'll start infusing growth factor drugs to restore my immunity. In the ensuing weeks, the new risk is "graft vs. host disease" whereby the new stem cells may attack my body as a foreign entity (to them). With adult donors, this can be quite dramatic; in the words of one of my consultants, the stem cells may seek to turn the recipient's body into the one they have left behind. *Invasion of the Body Snatchers*, anyone? With umbilical cord blood, the stem cells have no "memory" of another body, which may reduce the likelihood or severity of any attack on my system.

From there on out, they administer prophylactic medications to ward off bacterial, viral, and fungal infections until the stem cells establish a new immune system. Mr. Hickman will be working overtime. I've already had as many as five different medications and fluids merging into the two external lines that merge into the internal central line for delivery into my bloodstream, and this may well be the protocol again post-transplant.

The whole process is intellectually intriguing; it requires a blend of science, art, and craft from a team of oncologists, nurses, infectious disease doctors, and other specialists as needed. I'd prefer to learn about it without my own skin in the game, but that's how it goes.

This is perhaps more than you wanted to know, but thanks for reading this far. As I've mentioned to several of you, composing these emails has become my way of making sense out of some unfamiliar, complex, and frightening events, and it helps to have a supportive audience for these ramblings.

As you no doubt know (or fear) by now, I'll keep you posted. Such a long missive deserves a concise finish; here it is.

Joke of the Day:

A neutron walks into a bar and orders a drink.

Upon being asked the price, the bartender responds, "For you? No charge."

Cheers,
Steve

Countdown on Hold
October 6, 2016

Hi Again,

If you are about my age, you may remember those dramatic Apollo missions that became even more dramatic when they had to halt the countdown to solve an unexpected problem.

Well, after checking into the hospital this morning and landing one of the few west-facing, river-viewing, sunset-watching rooms, I had my first visit from the doctor. I felt obliged to report that Sue had developed cold symptoms on Tuesday and that despite my wearing a mask and sleeping in a separate room, I had noticed some potential cold symptoms myself upon awakening this morning.

The doctor asked some questions about my symptoms and decided to err on the side of caution, cancel the admission, and send me back home until it was clear whether I have a viral infection or not. He then related a story from his early days when they admitted a patient with cold symptoms for a transplant. After administering chemo and suppressing his immune system, the patient's cold developed into pneumonia and he died. As disappointed as I was to return home, I found this an extremely convincing rationale for his decision.

New plan: report to the clinic on Monday to assess whether I (still?) have an upper respiratory infection. If not, I expect admission to the hospital on Tuesday and the resumption of a countdown. If I am sick, we'll wait it out and then proceed when I'm infection-free.

In the last day, I have received over a dozen emails and several phone calls from many of you wishing me well as I turn this corner. I really appreciate those messages and will revisit them on the next evening before my next admission.

Unfortunately, the joke department is still returning inventory from the hospital, so this message *is* no joke and *has* no joke till we meet again.

Practicing being a patient patient,

Cheers,
Steve

Countdown Resumes
October 12, 2016

Hi All,

As you may recall, last week I had the world's shortest hospital admission. How do you flunk hospital admission in less than two hours? Here's how: tell the doctor you have possible cold symptoms that could complicate the procedure you're about to undergo. The doctor cited prudence and sent me home to see what would develop. He made a good call. Over the next few days, I weathered some garden-variety cold symptoms and a minor fever.

I was seen in the clinic on Monday when they ruled out the 4 strains of flu already active in the Twin Cities, as well as a bunch of other bad stuff. I returned to the clinic today, and the consensus is that the infection has been vanquished by my still-operative immune system. To be sure, they did a chest X-ray and the resulting image was even a tad better than the one they did during my work-up week. So all looks good.

As a result, the countdown resumes with the hospital admission tomorrow, followed by conditioning chemo and radiation. If everything stays on schedule, that should lead to the transplant a week from tomorrow and whatever further adventures await me after that.

I'll be re-reading all the good wishes I received on the

eve of my first admission and taking heart from them once again, but this time I'll try not to flunk out.

I'll send updates once I'm settled in.

Cheers,
Steve

4. The Stem Cell Adventure (Saved by a Baby)

"How do people tell stories when they are unsure of the experience they are trying to tell?"
—Arthur Frank, from *The Wounded Storyteller*

The following reports were composed from mid-October to early November of 2016. They describe the preparations for the transplant as well as the transplant itself. They also detail the shifting and unpredictable timetable about my discharge, as my doctors juggled the competing risks of leaving too early and needing a re-admission versus staying too long and contracting a hospital-borne infection that would further complicate my status.

Day -7
October 13, 2016

Hi All,

When I arrived at the hospital, there was a handwritten note on the shuttered door of the admissions department saying they were closed…and to report to the ER for admission. It turns out that the ubiquitous EPIC medical records system had crashed, and every record of every action for every patient has been hand-written all day long. As you may imagine, this makes for some unhappy nurses, but they're coping well.

Despite that inauspicious beginning, things have gone well. When I arrived on my floor, I requested one of the rare, west-facing rooms (4 out of 30 on the ward) and was told they were all full and it was not possible. I landed in a decent room with a southwest-facing, partial view of the river.

However, after chatting up my nurse about a room change and hearing of an unexpected discharge, I managed to snag one of those scarce rooms. I am now looking out a broad expanse of windows on the Mississippi River flowing from northeast to southwest. It's a great view except for the blinding afternoon sunlight which eventually gives way to a sunset over the Minneapolis skyline. One of the many things I have learned in my various hospital stays is that my spirit responds very positively to afternoon/evening light, so I couldn't be more pleased with my "campsite" for the next few weeks.

Tomorrow I begin five days of chemo (days -6 through -2), followed by one day of radiation (day -1), culminating in the transplant (day 0). On that day, they will transplant two bags of cord blood sequentially. They were selected because they are good matches. The stem cells happen to come from an infant boy and girl, so gender balance is being maintained throughout the process.

In a playful moment, I have christened my donors "Ralph" and "Gwen" respectively. Another factoid: 90% of the time, one cord will vanquish the other, but 10% of the time they both manage to coexist for an indefinite period. Ain't medical science interesting?

The joke inventory has just arrived, so we can close with the joke.

Joke of the Day:
E-flat walks into a bar.
The bartender immediately holds up his hand and says, "I'm sorry, you'll have to leave. We don't serve minors."

Cheers,
Steve

Day -3
October 17, 2016

Hi All,

Things are proceeding on schedule and I don't think there's any stopping the countdown now. I'm well through my double chemo regimen. Next up, the full body radiation on day -1. The goal is to kill any remaining cancer cells that have avoided detection by the prior biopsies and to wipe out my immune system, so it does not attack the graft being transplanted on day 0 (Thursday).

Today, they added two anti-rejection medications to create an even more hospitable environment for the incoming stem cells. Hopefully, they will find my body a nice place to inhabit and will engraft on schedule. The anti-rejection meds will continue for some weeks to maximize the chances that everybody gets along.

The day after the transplant, the nurses will start me on growth factor drugs to bring my immune system temporarily back on line to provide some defense against infection. Eventually, "my" immune system will give way to the new one being created by the transplant, but this bridging immunity may keep some infections at bay. As the graft implants and comes up to speed, they will monitor for "graft vs. host disease" and treat accordingly.

It's quite a process. Most of the doctors and nurses have

years of experience dealing with precisely this procedure, so I am reassured that they are prepared for almost any contingency. It doesn't eliminate the inherent risks of the procedure, but it does provide some peace of mind for me.

While my story remains positive, Sue's is less so. Although she has gradually become more mobile with recovery from her femur surgery, we are increasingly concerned about some cognitive or neurological issues that have become more prominent. This is a well-known side effect of fibromyalgia and this could also result from the narcotic painkillers she uses to control her body pain or interactive drug effects. Or it could be some new, undiagnosed cause.

With me in the hospital, her vulnerability living at home has become more concerning. We had recruited neighbors who agreed to be on call to help Sue during this time, and she may still call on them. What we need to clarify, however, is whether her condition requires assistance above and beyond what we can reasonably ask of our good neighbors. We hope to know that soon.

With her sister's help, she visited her doctor today. She received a referral for an MRI tomorrow and a follow-up visit with a neurology clinic. That may culminate in more extensive and professional home care. Her doctor has written a referral (yet to be approved by insurance) to a facility that can deal with this issue; we will see.

On a practical note, if you have experience with any of the medical alert or life alert systems that people living alone can use to contact emergency help, I'd appreciate any recommendations as to brand, company, type of service, etc.

Although this news is concerning, part of how I keep my spirits up is by regaling (torturing?) you with my sense of humor. So, we will honor tradition with the joke.

Joke of the Day:
A destitute man walks into a bar.

He settles on a stool and asks the bartender if he can have a line of credit to order a drink or two.

The bartender points out a sign behind the bar that reads "Our credit manager is Mrs. Helen C. Waite. If you want credit, go to Helen Waite."

Cheers,
Steve

P. S. Credit for this joke goes to Sue. When we first met, she took me to a hamburger joint named Solly's in Milwaukee run by a bevy of sweet, matronly ladies who slathered everything they cooked in butter and covered the walls of the joint with cheesy pastel paintings and corny plaques and sayings. However, when you took your check to the register, the credit policy above was spelled out in fancy calligraphy within a flowery, embroidered border. The message was quite a contrast with the ambience of the place, which made it memorable.

Day 0: Three's a Crowd
October 20, 2016

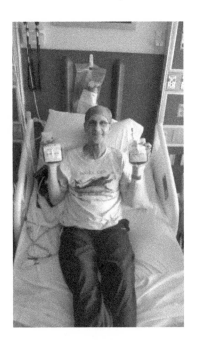

Hi All,

So, the deed has been done. Whitman said, "I contain multitudes." Well, I'm no Whitman, but I do have a couple new guests on board. Gwen and Ralph were "transplanted" from approximately 12:40 PM till 1:10 PM CDT on October 20 (Day Zero).

I had been drowsy all morning and so was compliant for the process. I received prophylactic diphenhydramine HCI and acetaminophen to moderate possible reactions to the preservatives used to maintain the integrity of the cord blood. During the procedure, I reported to the nurse some slight flushing and warmth, but otherwise tolerated the transplant with no complications.

Through a scientifically random process (the bag the nurse happened to grab first), Gwen was infused before Ralph. This led to an interesting discussion with my posse about whether we could count on Gwen to establish a nurturing, supportive atmosphere before Ralph arrived and just wanted to set up a man cave. This was heading toward a complex rehash of the hoary old "nature vs. nurture" debate, but I dozed off before the debate could get going.

I took pictures of the proceedings, including my transplant posse, a sophisticated pictorial flow chart of the procedure, and my opportunity to hold Ralph and Gwen before transplant. This last picture is reproduced here to introduce you to the kids I hope will save my life.

More good news. Just before the transplant, I spoke with Sue and learned that her brain scan MRI was completely positive and normal. This turns the speculation back to side effects and interactions of current medications as the most likely source of the cognitive challenges. There's more to learn, but that's a very reassuring result. So here is the joke.

Joke of the Day:
A guy walks into a bar and finds a horse serving drinks.
The horse asks, "What are you staring at? Haven't you ever seen a horse tending bar before?"

The guy says, "It's not that. I never thought the parrot would sell the place."

Cheers,
Steve

Hello, Neutropenia.
Can Thrombocytopenia be Far Behind?
October 24, 2016

Hi All,

On day 4 post-transplant, everything is proceeding as expected. My white blood cell, neutrophil, and platelet counts are bottoming out as a predictable side-effect of the previous chemo. My vulnerability to infection will peak over the next ten days, but no nasty stuff has occurred so far.

The last few days have brought a couple of challenges and some apparent solutions. My chemo regimen has led to my loss of appetite and nausea. For a day or two, the thought of food was quite repulsive. Then they "turned me on" to an appetite booster and nausea control medication. It's a synthetic derivative of marijuana; they somehow remove the *high*, but I still got the munchies. It doesn't give me a ravenous appetite, but it flips a switch so food is appealing again. I'm eating normally with careful timing of the drug.

I've also experienced two mornings of an "altered state" that starts with blurry vision (a known side effect of the anti-fungal medication I am taking). It then generalizes to dizziness/balance issues, a foggy mind, disorientation, mood swings, and lethargy. My doctor and nurses all asked if I am having hallucinations, and I am not. They get really excited at the prospect of hallucinating patients, so I was sorry to disappoint them.

Since this condition mimicked a mildly unpleasant drug experience, I asked the nurses if we could administer the (supposedly inert) anti-nausea drug and the anti-fungal medication several hours apart rather than simultaneously. Today is the first day they have implemented my request, and my symptoms are already noticeably better.

Looking forward, they are continuing to give me two anti-rejection medications as well as a growth factor medication to bring my white blood cells back on line sooner rather than later. *If* my counts (which have yet to hit bottom) were to recover quickly and strongly, there is a remote chance they would send me home in just a couple of weeks on the theory that remaining in the hospital is riskier than living (carefully) in the world, as long as my immunity holds and no infections occur.

It's much more likely I will still be here on day 21 (Thursday, Nov. 10) when they will do a biopsy to determine if the graft has taken hold. If not, I'm not sure what happens. Graft failure is only a 10% risk. If engraftment happens, counts recover, and there is little to no graft-vs.-host-disease, I could be discharged any time.

Meanwhile, my brother Jerome arrived this past weekend on a mission of mercy from Wisconsin. He visited me on Saturday (with Sue) and Sunday, then stayed at the house to help Sue with various chores. In addition, Sue seems back to her old self after the bumpy start last week.

Finally, for those of you with long memories, we may be close to getting our deck repaired from the July 5 storm. Fortunately, the roof and gutters were replaced promptly, but various issues have slowed the deck repairs. We might call it contractor-vs.-insurance company disease. Nonetheless, we hope to have all new railings up in time for the first snowfall.

On that note, we present the joke.

Joke of the Day:

A gorilla walks into a bar and says, "A scotch on the rocks, please." The gorilla hands the bartender a $10 bill.

The bartender thinks to himself, *this gorilla doesn't know the prices of drinks,* and gives him 15 cents change.

The bartender says, "You know, we don't get too many gorillas in here."

The gorilla replies, "Well, at $9.85 a drink, I ain't coming back, either."

Cheers,
Steve

Twists and Turns in the Road
October 30, 2016

Hi All,

This adventure is nothing, if not surprising. For my first two weeks, I've avoided virtually all post-chemo side-effects, post-transplant complications, and any need for transfusions of platelets or red blood cells. In the words of my attending doctor, I have become known as the rock star on my ward for my smooth progress through this process. (I did have a four-year career as a drummer in college, but drummers are rarely "stars").

So, although I was told beforehand to expect a hospital stay of anywhere between three and six weeks, last Friday I was told to prepare for a Monday discharge, which would get me out of here in a mere two and a half weeks.

Then on Saturday, my temperature went above the critical benchmark of 100.5 F. With that temperature, they assumed there was an infection and requested a chest X-ray, a urine sample, and blood for blood cultures to try and grow the critters in the lab. They also started me on an additional IV antibiotic. While acetaminophen brought the fever down, it spiked again at 2 AM and 4 PM on Sunday. With fevers on two consecutive days, the staff is becoming more serious about discovering the cause. The practical outcome is that the earliest I would be discharged would be next Wednesday. Not surprisingly, the doctor did *not* refer to me today as the rock star of the ward, so it was a brief career.

If my white blood cell counts continue to drop (after a spike when I started the growth factor medication), I may become neutropenic again and that will prolong my stay. A common pattern is for the host's few remaining white blood cells to get a jolt from the growth factor drugs and the numbers to go up dramatically. But then, it's done. It's like the finale as the fireworks conclude. Then the old system is off line and the new system needs a bit more time to engraft and produce its own cells. The result is that I'll probably face another period of heightened vulnerability due to low counts, until Gwen and Ralph seriously get to work. And all that would return the process to the original estimate of four to five weeks of hospitalization.

Whenever I get out, I will continue with daily visits to the clinic for the first month so they can assess my status, adjust medications, provide transfusions, etc. I will be getting help from my brother and my buddy, Dave, who will provide live-in help in rotating weeks for the first month. After that, the frequency of clinic visits should taper off and we'll improvise how to get that done.

The longer-term challenge is to watch for signs of "graft-vs.-host-disease" which usually occurs in about 60% of cases like mine. It can take a lot of different forms and will require prompt intervention to keep it under control. This is a good time for me to remember their admonition to see this as a 100-day marathon and today is only day 10. I've learned that if I take one day at a time, the days do seem to add up.

Joke of the Day:
A priest, a rabbi, a minister, and an imam walk into a bar.

The bartender looks at them and says, "What is this, a joke?"

Cheers,
Steve

Day 14 Update
November 3, 2016

Hi All,

I thought it might be time for a quick update. The fevers I mentioned in my 10/30 email persisted until last night in a highly predictable pattern. For five afternoons and four nights, the fevers peaked within about an hour on either side of 3 PM and 2 AM respectively. They responded to meds, but it was a lot of body aches and chills every twelve hours for five days.

I may be a bit weird, but I often don't know how bad I'm feeling until I feel better. A recovery from pain or other symptoms gives me a fresh, new basis of comparison to retroactively realize I had felt crummy before I felt better. Maybe that's a psychological defense mechanism, but I fall for it every time.

The pattern finally broke yesterday afternoon, with just low-grade fevers or normal temps. They've run a variety of tests and scans to identify the infectious agent, but all that has been found so far is an upper respiratory infection, so I have a common cold with the standard symptoms. They continue searching for bacterial, viral, or fungal sources of infection, but the fever could also be a side-effect of the grafting process (a good thing) and/or the growth factor drugs I'm taking to spur the formation of white blood cells.

I have also developed a rash—another side-effect of the grafting process itself or of the many medications I am taking. They are treating it with a steroid cream and it's under control for now. Other than that, I'm tolerating the procedures and medications fairly well.

My counts continue to drop in small amounts each day, but the staff is anticipating a turnaround soon as the stem cells engraft and begin doing their magic. The discharge criteria remains the same: no fever for an extended period and counts adequate to provide at least minimal immunity. No one is placing bets on a specific day (or even week), so it's back to that waiting game.

The next significant scheduled event is a bone marrow biopsy one week from today. Hopefully, it will provide evidence of engraftment and that things are heading in the right direction. That's it for now, except for the joke.

Joke of the Day:
Two peanuts walked into a bar; one was assaulted.

Cheers,
Steve

Jailbreak
November 7, 2016

Hi All,

The stars have aligned. I've had no fevers for almost a week, most of my symptoms are gone or well-controlled, and my white blood cell and neutrophil counts are steadily trending up. At this point, remaining in the hospital is riskier than going home. They are discharging me tomorrow, barring any fever or infection in the next eighteen hours or so.

My brother will arrive from Wisconsin tomorrow morning in time for a couple of teaching sessions for patients and caregivers as I transition from inpatient to outpatient. He will drive me home after my three-week, five-day hospital stay—not bad when they were predicting anywhere from three to six weeks.

We will return to the clinic the very next morning for my blood draws, medication adjustments, or needed transfusions, and that will be the routine for the next several weeks. However, Thursday's clinic visit will bring the added excitement of a bone marrow biopsy that should confirm that engraftment is occurring. They may be able to measure how much of me is still me, Gwen, or Ralph based on our respective DNA traces.

That said, I'm leaving on only day 19 of a 100-day journey, and there are still serious potential risks if/when "graft vs. host disease" sets in. That's the best reason for the 24/7 caregiver role for the first month. If there's evidence of GVHD, I may need to be treated quickly to keep it in check.

Still, I'm very pleased with my progress. The staff here tells me that they have trouble getting most patients out of bed during their second and third week post-transplant. With the exception of two rough days last week, I have maintained my stretching/exercise/yoga/treadmill routines, and I feel well-positioned to make this transition to home. So, without further ado, here is the joke.

Joke of the Day:

A cowboy walks into a bar and orders a beer. His hat is made of brown wrapping paper, his shirt and vest are made of waxed paper, and his chaps, pants, and boots are made of tissue paper.

Soon, they arrest him for rustling.

Cheers,
Steve

5. Home for Good (Adult and Baby are Doing Fine)

"Telling stories of illness is the attempt, instigated by the body's disease, to give a voice to an experience that medicine cannot describe."
—Arthur Frank, from *The Wounded Storyteller*

These reports were composed from mid-November of 2016 to late April of 2017. They cover a longer span of time and gradually became less frequent as there was less "breaking news" to report. The reports discuss a challenging first month at home when the undesirable side-effects of the transplant were most evident. After that, it's a story of gradual improvement and recovery with occasional regressions and bumps in the road before culminating in my day 180 biopsy and consult.

Home Sweet Home
November 15, 2016

Hi All,

So, it's been seven days since my jailbreak from the hospital and things are going well at home.

The new routine involves taking a combination of up to twelve drugs on differing schedules throughout the day. I have an elaborate spreadsheet and a pill box the size of a small Buick, but it's well-organized under the watchful eye of my caregivers. The medications themselves include antibiotic, antiviral and antifungal pills, two different anti-rejection medications, two anti-nausea medications, and a couple pills to counteract some of the side effects of the other pills.

I'm also making daily clinic visits with my caretaker that begin with a blood draw. My counts are beginning to come up, but I am still receiving a growth factor injection at the clinic to spur the recovery of even more white blood cells. Depending on my counts, the staff may keep me longer at any clinic visit to transfuse platelets (which I've needed the last five days and takes an hour to infuse) or red blood cells (which I haven't needed but will take an additional two hours if/when I do). I've worked to get non-rush hour appointment times, but even with that, any given appointment can take as little as two or as much as six hours out of the day.

During my clinic visit last Thursday, I had a bone marrow biopsy to detect any lingering cancer cells and to measure how much engraftment has already begun. This coming Thursday, I have my 28 day "anniversary" appointment with my oncologist, to get the results.

Since coming home, I have experienced a slight uptick in nausea, some notable body and bone aches, and levels of fatigue that I have never experienced before. Think rag doll. Doing simple household chores can be a challenge, and the degree of muscle deconditioning is unsettling.

On the upside, all this is not only consistent with, but indicative of, a successful engraftment process that is underway but leaving me with little energy. Engraftment means there are lots of juvenile white blood cells (I think they roam in gangs) looking for trouble in my body and seizing on any muscle, bone, or joint that has ever been injured and trying to repair it, even though it's already healed. Their overly enthusiastic if well intentioned efforts account for much of the pain I'm having.

As the engraftment proceeds, my new immune system should get better at discriminating between real threats (including any lingering leukemia) and old stuff that doesn't require attention. And at some point, I may get some version of graft-vs.-host disease, but so far, so good.

The fatigue is consistent with my low red blood cell count, which limits my ability to oxygenate muscles and maintain strength. In the last couple of days, however, those symptoms have moderated. I have also found ways to treat, medicate, or otherwise blunt their most uncomfortable aspects. Then I feel good enough to keep up with my stretching/exercise/yoga routines that are more important than ever to rebuild my strength.

Yesterday was a test of the inner-circle caregiving team I've assembled. My brother has been here since my discharge last Tuesday, so he dropped me at the clinic at noon on Monday, and headed back to Wisconsin, his family, and job. Meanwhile, Dave was making his way up from Milwaukee to my house to be my caregiver this week. When my clinic visit was over, I called my local utility-infielder caregiver, Tom, who took me home. Dave had just arrived and was getting settled in.

So, within a three-hour period, I was under the sequential care of all three of my inner circle caregivers, and the plan was executed without a hitch, just like we drew it up in practice. Dave will be with me throughout this week. Then Jerome returns for the next handoff this coming Sunday.

For obvious reasons, Sue and I are both happy I'm home. We're developing a three-way system of everybody helping with cooking, laundry, and cleaning, as time and energy permits. Given some of my levels of fatigue, I'm very happy to have two people who can assist with things. Thanks to everybody's effort, the home-based caregiving system is working well.

Big picture, this has been a significant and positive week in my recovery and it deserves a quality finish. For those of you who appreciated the joke about the Italian policeman trying to purchase two croissants, I think you will find the same high quality and warped sense of humor in today's entry from my Italian friend and correspondent, Bruna. Hence, we proudly present our second, trans-Atlantic joke.

Joke of the Day:
A new client walks into a bar in Veneto and orders a spritz with two olives.

The bartender prepares it and the man drinks the spritz, takes the two olives, and rolls them into his ears. He then pays and leaves.

The bartender is very perplexed but doesn't dare ask anything.

The next day the client reappears, orders the same, and repeats the operation.

This goes on for five days, while the bartender keeps thinking about how to address the issue. Finally, he gets an idea.

When the client reappears on the sixth day and makes

the same order, the bartender apologizes. "Sorry sir, I ran out of olives. I only have pickles today."

The client doesn't seem disappointed. He drinks the spritz, rolls the two pickles in his ears, and prepares to pay and leave.

At this point the bartender explodes, "Why in the hell did you roll the two pickles into your ears?"

The client, equally upset, says, "What do you mean, why did I put the pickles into my ears? You just told me you ran out of olives!"

Cheers,
Steve

A Shadow of my Former Self
November 18, 2016

Hi All,

Yesterday was day 28 post-transplant and I met with my oncologist about the results of my day 21 bone marrow biopsy. The news is all good.

First, as expected, the biopsy shows no signs of residual leukemia. While this method cannot detect every possible pocket of lingering cancer cells, it's as good a measure and outcome as we can have at this point.

Second, and less expected, there is strong evidence of successful and virtually complete engraftment. Based on the DNA analysis of the tissue from the biopsy, I am now 99% Ralph and 1% me. It's best not to ask about Gwen at this point.

As I understood the conversation, this is unusually early for such a complete result. It's the kind of outcome they expect when they do a full intensity transplant for folks under age 55 and wipe out all their bone marrow with wickedly high doses of chemo and radiation.

In my case, they did an age-appropriate, reduced intensity transplant with less chemo and radiation which was expected to leave roughly 10-15% of my bone marrow intact for the time being. Again, if I'm hearing this correctly, this means that Ralph has not only established himself, but has cleaned up my remaining bone marrow and any potential sources of lingering cancer. I have the ideal outcome of the riskier procedure with the lesser risks of the reduced intensity procedure. How cool is that?

This means I can eliminate a couple of medications (that may be contributing to my side effects of nausea, aches, and fatigue) while adding one to prevent new problems. There is still a risk of GVHD where Ralph may attack my healthy parts until he learns better. Another big concern is pneumonia, which affects many patients in the next 30-60-day period, so I will be juggling drugs to prevent that risk. Daily clinic visits will continue for now, although I may get a day or two off in the coming weeks as things continue to stabilize.

Speaking of clinic visits, I must get ready for today's appointment, so I will leave you with the joke.

Joke of the Day:
Charles Dickens walks into a bar and orders a martini. The bartender asks, "Olive or Twist?"

Cheers,
Steve

Day 39 Report
November 28, 2016

Hi All,

Well, it's been a quiet week here in Lake Wobegon. The only bump in my road arose on a clinic visit about a week ago when I was informed that the docs had detected the cytomegalovirus in my system through a routine blood analysis. That prompted a change in my antiviral medication to target this specific critter. Interestingly, this virus is present in over half of all adults but held in check by a healthy immune system. When immunocompromised, the virus can become active and require treatment.

Among its effects, the virus drives down white blood cell counts, so my gradual progress in building up from 2.2 to 6.6 over nine days was wiped out as the count dropped back to 2.2 in a single day. The antiviral medication also suppresses white blood cell counts, so I was concerned about how low this would go.

Apparently, the medication was effective and its suppressive effects minor, as my WBC rose from 2.4 to 10.1 in just two days. My hemoglobin and platelets also continue to increase, so I have not needed a transfusion in a week. For the few days when the virus was active, I had elevated symptoms of fatigue, aches, chills, and nausea, but they are all qualitatively better in the last two days.

After first leaving the hospital, I had clinic visits every day for ten days, then had a day off. Then I had only three appointments last week and hopefully only two this week. That's a good score compared to the expectation that I would have daily clinic visits every day for a month.

The 24/7 caregiving team continues to function flawlessly, with Jerome, Dave, Jerome again and now Donna taking weekly hitches. Jerome will return this coming weekend for one more tour of duty. The handoffs take place mostly on Sunday when someone arrives from Wisconsin and the current caregiver heads for home.

Sue is also doing well enough to take on extra chores that I might normally do, allowing me to rest as needed and still get some activity when I feel up to it.

One piece of advice I received before this all started is that this is a marathon and not a sprint, and to realize that you can't rush the process. That's helpful to remember when things feel like Groundhog Day, with every day starting with a bunch of pills, trying to maintain an exercise program, taking more pills, doing some minimal chores, taking naps, and then ending the day taking more pills. That said, I should note that, depending on which caregiver is in town, there have been some memorable three-handed games of sheepshead or pinochle played.

With hopes that everyone had a good Thanksgiving, we close with the joke.

Joke of the Day:
Several fonts walk into a bar.
"Get out of here!" shouts the bartender. "We don't serve your type here."

Cheers,
Steve

A Fork in the Road?
December 6, 2016

Hi All,

Yesterday brought another flawless hand-off by team Wisconsin, as Donna dropped me at my noon clinic appointment and headed back to the Badger state while Jerome arrived at the clinic promptly at 12:30, before I was even called for the blood draw that initiates all my appointments.

Jerome will stay through my Thursday appointment and then head home, marking the retirement of team Wisconsin after four and a half weeks of highly coordinated, three-handed, multi-skilled, unfailingly cheerful, sheepshead and pinochle playing, 24/7 support. They have been terrific, and I can't thank them enough.

This is day 47 and things still look good with one possible exception—every good story needs a little drama. The aches and chills of previous weeks have receded, while the mild nausea and fatigue continue. The nausea is manageable, and while the fatigue seems constant, I must remind myself that I am increasing my activity daily without any increase in fatigue, so that can be read as a good sign as well.

From a clinical standpoint, the only thing catching my

doctors' attention is the cytomegalovirus which was diagnosed a couple weeks ago. They put me on a more targeted antiviral medication twice a day to treat it and planned to reduce the meds to a maintenance dose of once a day. However, the viral and antiviral forces have battled to a standstill, so I'm staying on the twice-a-day dosing for the time being.

In another week, we will face a fork in the road. Which reminds me; a famous baseball catcher once said if you come to a fork in the road, take it…but I digress. On the one hand, if the antiviral medication is effective in taming the virus, I may be able to drop to one clinic visit per week much earlier than we anticipated, greatly easing the clinic transportation challenge in the absence of team Wisconsin.

On the other hand, if the virus is still prominent despite the oral medications, they will want me to go back into the hospital for a short time to receive more intensive IV antiviral medications to vanquish the cytomegalovirus for good. I'm obviously rooting for fork one, but I would grudgingly accept a limited hospital stay for a specific purpose to get the virus behind me.

Other than that, no signs of infection, serious side-effects, complications, or GVHD so far. Another mark of improvement is that after almost ten consecutive days of platelet transfusions ending a couple weeks ago, "I" now seem to be producing "my" own platelets at a rapid pace. That's good on the face of it, but it is also another sign of successful engraftment; i. e., it's really Ralph who has the platelet division working overtime.

All in all, good news, with reason to keep fingers crossed. This is a time when good advice is at a premium, so here is some in the form of the joke.

Joke of the Day:
Jack Handy walks in to a bar.

The bartender recognizes him as the writer of a 1990s Saturday Night Live segment called "Deep Thoughts by Jack Handy."

The bartender asks Jack what his favorite "deep thought" was.

Without hesitation, Jack slips into that sonorous yet mellifluous New-Age voice and intones, "Sometimes in life, other people will get under our skin and we will be tempted to criticize them. But always remember, before you criticize someone, first walk a mile in their shoes. That way, when you criticize them, you're a mile away and you have their shoes."

Cheers,
Steve

A Third Fork: The Road Taken
December 16, 2016

Hi All,

In my last note of 12/6, I was facing a fork in the road: either my cytomegalovirus had to respond more quickly to oral antiviral medications or I would have to go back to the hospital as an inpatient to receive IV medications.

Since then, two good things have happened. First, the virus began to lose out to the antiviral medications. Second, that allowed us to do an *outpatient* infusion of IV immunoglobulin to vanquish the virus for good. They warned me the infusion could take up to four hours, but once they knew I was tolerating it well, they sped it up so I finished it in a little under three hours—just enough time to read three chapters in T. C. Boyle's new novel *Terranauts* and solve two Sudoku puzzles.

The weekend before this Monday infusion, however, I developed a new symptom: intermittent shortness of breath upon mild exertion. I spoke with an on-call doctor on Sunday and we agreed it was a close call between coming in to the emergency room that day or waiting till my regular Monday clinic visit. Another fork in another road, eh?

The problem was that the (literal) roads to the U of M ER were still receiving snow in near zero temperatures that turned the freeways into a cross between a parking lot and a demolition derby. Once again, a third fork came to mind.

Rather than doing nothing or driving to the distant and dangerous-to-reach ER, we went to our local urgent care where a chest X-ray and an EKG ruled out fluid in the lungs or unusual stresses on the heart. They couldn't rule out a blood clot in my lungs because that required a CT scan machine they didn't have, but after discussing my symptoms in greater detail, I decided to wait until Monday's scheduled clinic visit.

Long story, short: Monday's CT scan revealed no pulmonary issues, so the intermittent breathing issue bears watching, but is probably due to the cumulative effect of all the meds I've been taking, along with the virus (which is now on the run) as well as the antiviral medications.

Last, but not least, I'm experiencing some neuropathy in my feet. I first noticed a pinpoint of numbness months ago in one foot and then another, and assumed it was due to walking on tile and hardwood floors without sufficient padding. In the last month, those pinpoints have expanded to a larger radius of numbness. No pain, no tingling, just a dead zone, as if three layers of insensate sock material were bunched up under the ball of my foot. My chemo treatments and medications are suspect in this reaction, but I'm scheduled to see a podiatrist this afternoon to get more insight. If, however, you can offer a winning diagnosis before I see the doctor, you will win…whatever prize I can come up with.

The big picture is looking good. Aches and chills are gone, nausea is under control, fatigue is down, energy and activity levels are up, and my mind is a bit clearer as we reduce doses or eliminate some of the many medicines I've been taking since leaving the hospital. There are no indications of graft-vs.-host disease to date, which is a good sign at day 57 post-transplant.

Several people expressed appreciation of Jack Handy's deep thought (in which a pair of shoes played a crucial part) in my last email. In the interest of thematic continuity, shoes also play a crucial part in our new joke.

Joke of the Day:

An otherwise shabbily-dressed, homeless guy wearing a pair of Gucci loafers made of fine Italian leather walks into a bar.

The bartender asks, "How you doing?"

The guy says, "Better now, but I had some rough weeks." He proceeds to describe how he was so poor that he had no shoes and how depressed that made him feel.

"But then," he says, "I met a man who had no feet. Something like that can really change your perspective. So, I said to this man, 'Got any shoes you're not using?'."

Cheers,
Steve

My New Shoes Are No Joke
December 23, 2016

Hi All,

Well, it's day 64 and my news continues to be mostly good.

Until January 16, I will remain on a maintenance dose of the antiviral medication that resolved my cytomegalovirus. One side-effect of that medication is to depress my white blood cell count, so I will also receive growth factor injections as needed during regular clinic visits to counteract that effect. They can make my numbers dance like puppets with all the tools at their disposal.

The other heavy-duty medication I remain on is cyclosporine, a standard anti-rejection drug. It's crucial to preventing or minimizing graft-vs.-host-disease, so it's probably my most important medication right now. Among its side-effects are numbness, tingling, and burning sensations in the hands or feet, so I thought I was on to something here that would explain my foot issues.

Meanwhile, I saw a podiatrist who diagnosed my problem as Morton's neuroma, which means pinched nerves behind the toes that produce numbness and may progress to chronic pain. It's possible that the cyclosporine has exacerbated this underlying condition, or even that my immature immune system is trying to repair a pre-existing

151

injury and making it worse. Or it could be a separate issue independent of the cancer/chemo/drugs/immune system nexus. As with many things, time will tell.

My podiatrist recommended a "house shoe" or clog made by Haflinger to minimize my discomfort. Reflecting fine German engineering, this shoe features high arch support, a metatarsal pad, and a deep, wide toe box. The shoe takes pressure off the sensitive areas and provides plenty of room for toes and nerves. If you have a foot problem akin to mine, you need to check out this shoe. It's why, despite the jokes in my last two emails, my new shoes are no joke.

The departure of Team Wisconsin several weeks ago posed new challenges in getting clinic rides. My thanks to Team Minnesota for getting me there and back the week of the 12th. Last Friday, I decided to cross a line and drove myself to my podiatrist appointment. That went well, so I drove to both of my downtown clinic visits this past Monday and Thursday.

By doing this, I'm technically in violation of the "no driving in the first 100 days" and "never be without a caregiver" injunctions. Having violated the conditions of my parole, I offer this defense.

First, my recovery has been more rapid than expected; second, I have learned how my medications affect me (e. g., don't take the vision-blurring voriconazole before driving to the clinic); and third, my energy, mind, and focus are all better since eliminating some prior medications. All in all, reclaiming this measure of independence feels right at this juncture. I also don't have to tax the generosity of my neighbors and friends for rides, although several of them have agreed to be "on call" on future days when I may not be up to driving.

If all goes well next week, we may be able to drop back to one clinic visit per week through day 100. That would be nice, but as always, everything is dependent on remaining free of infection and GVHD. So far, so good. With best wishes for whichever and however you celebrate your holidays, we present the joke.

Joke of the Day:

Two cartons of yogurt walk into a bar.

The bartender, who is a tub of cottage cheese, says to them, "We don't serve your kind in here."

One of the yogurt cartons says to him, "Why not? We're cultured individuals."

Cheers,
Steve

My Year in Review: By the Numbers
December 30, 2016

Hi All,

At yesterday's clinic visit, I saw Tasha, one of my favorite physician assistants. She walked into the room saying, "Your counts are good. Let me listen to your heart and lungs, and then get you out of here so you don't have to come back for a week." I'm now down to only one clinic visit per week, with a month to go till day 100.

The big picture remains good: no fevers, infections, or graft-vs.-host disease. The small picture is stable: lingering fatigue, intermittent nausea, and foot numbness. While I'm not out of the woods yet, I can't argue with this status after a procedure with a 20% mortality rate and a 60% chance of GVHD.

That said, a certain tedium has nonetheless set in after seventy plus days of being hospital- or house-bound, except for clinic visits. It's like having a Groundhog Day syndrome where each day feels like a repeat of the one before. It doesn't *feel* like I'm making the progress I know I really am.

That sense of stasis led me to revisit my path over the last six months. As a sociologist, I'm always interested in data, facts, and scientific inquiry—even if it is out of fashion these days. As a home-bound cancer patient, perhaps I have a bit too much time on my hands.

In any event, I have compiled a numerical summary of some randomly chosen items over the last 6+ months. Here's the data for the period starting on June 15. Some numbers are "best estimates".

167 Days since diagnosis

73 Days in hospitals (2 hospitals; 4 separate admissions)

1 Hickman central line surgically implanted for blood draws/infusions

4 Chemotherapy drugs delivered over three treatment cycles

1 Dose of full body radiation

1 Colitis/E-coli infection (due to post-chemo immunosuppression)

1 Full body rash (due to post-chemo immunosuppression)

1 Cytomegalovirus (due to post-chemo immunosuppression)

2 U of M consultations regarding stem cell transplant

2 Second opinions regarding stem cell transplant from Mayo Clinic

2 Umbilical cord blood samples used in transplant

100 % engraftment of male umbilical cord stem cells (aka "Ralph")

71 Days since stem cell transplant

4 EKG tests

6 X-rays

1 MRI

2 Ultrasounds

8 CT scans

1 Pulmonary Function Test

1 MUGA Cardiac Function Test

1 Lumbar Puncture

1 Immunoglobulin Infusion

17 Platelet Transfusions

3 Red Blood Cell Transfusions

2 Dermatological Biopsies

6 Bone Marrow Biopsies

725 Minutes on hold ordering meals during 25-day U of M hospital stay

13 Out-patient clinic visits (pre-transplant)

23 Out-patient clinic visits (post-transplant)

327 Vials of blood drawn for diagnostic purposes (inpatient and outpatient)

22 Medications prescribed at post-transplant discharge from hospital

6 Medications still taking

159 Yoga sessions

39 Get well cards received

14 Relatives, friends, and neighbors who provided material support

40 Mass emails w/jokes

For anyone who's had a serious bout with cancer (or knows someone who has), these data will not be surprising. I'm not claiming my experience is exceptional in any way, but it was certainly beyond my imagination until I found myself living it day-by-day and trying to roll with the punches.

So, I guess I *can* account for my time over the last six months after all. I've been feeling like not much has been happening. The data, however, reveal significant milestones and slow but steady progress.

Speaking of that, Sue's mobility has improved since her sacrum fracture last May and broken femur in June. Here's one indicator of how we know this. For months, she would ask for her cane *before* walking across the room, up the stairs, or across the parking lot. Now she walks across the room, up the stairs, or across the parking lot (and more) and says, "Oh, I guess I forgot my cane."

So, as this year comes to a close, we have reason for optimism for next year, and we wish the best for all of you as well. I couldn't come up with a new-year's-themed joke, so we delve into the realm of philosophy for today's joke.

Joke of the Day:

The French philosopher Rene Descartes walks into a bar.

The bartender says, "Hey Rene, what are you having?"

Descartes orders a Belgian ale and sits down to watch a soccer game.

About twenty minutes later, the attentive bartender asks Rene if he would like another beer.

Descartes responds, "I think not," and POOF. He vanishes into thin air.

Cheers and Happy New Year!
Steve & Sue

Mr. Hickman Gets the Boot
January 6, 2017

Hi All,

I've now gone a week between clinic visits. Yesterday's numbers were good with no need for infusions, transfusions, inhalations, or shots. I have future clinic visits on the 12th and 19th of January, and a bone marrow biopsy to confirm there is no residual cancer on January 27th (day 99). I will have my "anniversary visit" on February 2nd, just past the 100 day mark.

Yesterday my oncologist surprised me by saying we should remove my Hickman central line. The logic is that with only weekly blood draws, the risk of keeping the central line (getting an infection) is now greater than the cost of stabbing me with a needle once a week. Mr. Hickman has been with me since June 16th and was the pathway for the 327 vials of blood itemized in my last email. What I didn't mention was that for every outgoing blood draw, there were probably 4 or 5 incoming doses of chemo, meds, or fluids. Thus, Mr. Hickman came in very handy, and I thank him for his service.

In trying to schedule this procedure in conjunction with a clinic visit, I asked if I would be sedated and need a driver. I "confessed" that I have been driving myself (in violation of the 100-day ban) for the last two weeks but could get a driver if needed.

With great melodramatic timing, my oncologist looked at me, raised one eyebrow, and said, "I didn't hear that." As it happens, they hadn't realized the thing was implanted at my first hospital and needs to be removed by them. It's much closer to home, there will be no sedative, and I can drive myself to next Monday's appointment for the removal.

It will be nice to shower again without wrapping my upper torso in Saran Wrap to protect the gizmo.

So, I am making progress by several indicators, which prompted me to push a bit on when I could go somewhere other than clinic visits, be in crowds, not wear the mask, etc. I received the needed pushback and clarification about the 100-day rule. It's not a completely arbitrary number because that's the day they'll begin to taper down my anti-rejection medication. Up to now, my twice daily doses have been suppressing my immune system, even though my numbers look good. With the tapering of the anti-rejection medication after day 100, my immune system can gain some strength and offer some protection.

Put differently, while I'm on this medication, I'm as vulnerable to infection as the day I left the hospital and there should be no relaxation of the precautions I've been following all along. Or, as my oncologist put it, we'll have that conversation about relaxing the rules after day 100.

For added emphasis, she told a brief story of someone in my status who caught a virus most of you would fight off without noticing, but he ended up in the intensive care unit for ten days. I don't know how the story ended, but she had me at "intensive care unit." I regard this as a solid second opinion backing up my good friend Dave's advice from the start that I do everything I possibly can to avoid all sources of infection. Point taken, hunker down, shields up, until day 100.

For those of you here in the North, I hope you're enjoying our winter. For those of you elsewhere, it's not as bad as they say it is. Why is it "news" that it's cold in Minnesota in winter? Speaking of numbers, here's the joke.

Joke of the Day:
Infinitely many mathematicians walk into a bar.
The first says, "I'll have a beer."
The second says, "I'll have half a beer."
The third says, "I'll have a quarter of a beer."
Before anyone else can speak, the barman fills up exactly two glasses of beer and serves them. "Come on, now," he says to the group. "You guys have got to learn your limits."

Cheers,
Steve

Day 92 Status and Reflections
January 20, 2017

Hi All,

It's been a quiet two weeks since my last email. A week ago, there was some concern about my liver function numbers being a bit high. They anticipated changing some medications that could be contributing to the problem. Yesterday's numbers, however, were better, so that issue is resolved. I'm still scheduled for a bone marrow biopsy next Friday (day 99) and my "anniversary visit" to mark the end of my one-hundred days the following Thursday (actually day 105).

There are still no obvious signs of graft-vs.-host disease, which is welcome. I do have an odd collection of minor symptoms, including neuropathy in my feet, some minor rashes, dry eyes, and sinus headaches that have persisted for several days. These are all maladies that I experienced before my diagnosis and treatment, but they seem more intense and persistent than in the past.

My gut feeling is that these conditions were somehow controlled by my former immune system, but my new immune system (Ralph is three months old today!) has not quite learned how to achieve the same equilibrium. They could also be indirect side effects of the medications

I continue to take. When I mentioned this to the doctors, they acknowledge my logic but caution that it's mere speculation until I get off these medications and Ralph has a chance to mature.

During these quiet weeks, I've had time to process this experience and realize how unusual my journey has been. For instance, there are ongoing discussions in the medical community about how to describe people with cancer. Am I a cancer patient, a cancer victim, a cancer survivor, or some other designation? I'm less concerned about the second word than the first, in that I have not been able to easily connect my experiences with my preconceptions of cancer.

From the beginning, and despite my diagnosis, I never felt as if I "had" cancer. That may sound odd, but consider the history. I was completely asymptomatic upon my diagnosis; I felt fine, normal, and healthy. I have felt anything but fine over the last seven months, but there is not a single subjective, somatic condition that I can connect to the cancer itself. Every abnormal symptom I have had can be directly attributed to chemotherapy, radiation, the immunosuppression my treatment created, or the myriad medications I've taken. Moreover, even these reactions have been blessedly mild (no pain, minimal nausea, etc.)

The upshot is that I don't easily relate to the term (or the cultural connotations of) "cancer." Throughout this time, I have also felt and looked healthier than most of the other cancer patients I have seen in hospitals and at clinic visits. I simply don't feel like I am part of the cancer community and the undeniably supportive resources to be found there.

Maybe this is equal parts naiveté, denial, and defense mechanism, but the upshot is that I feel incredibly lucky and grateful to be where I am, given my initial diagnosis some seven months ago.

While I don't in any way deny my diagnosis, I can imagine a compelling medical thriller in the hands of the right novelist. Begin with the premise that the profit-driven, cancer-pharmaceutical complex needs a continual flow of "patients." One strategy to accomplish this would be to show healthy people test "results" that indicate "cancer" that require immediate and expensive treatment, and that novices are not easily able to challenge.

Multiply this scam by thousands of cases daily, and voila: the census of cancer patients is kept at a profitable level. Call it goofy, far-fetched, or paranoid, but in the hands of a Stephen King or the late Michael Crichton, can you envision a best-selling work of fiction? Maybe it's something to occupy me in my upcoming retirement.

Enough rambling. Since I'm pondering some existential issues here, I offer this as a fitting joke.

Joke of the Day:

The ghost of George Carlin walks into a bar.

The bartender pours him a nice merlot and asks how he's been.

Carlin's ghost says he's good, and his experience with the afterlife has taught him the difference between heaven and hell.

Intrigued by this, the bartender asks him to elaborate.

Carlin's ghost draws this distinction:

In Heaven...

The Italians are the lovers,

The French cook the food,

The Swiss run the hotels,

The Germans are the mechanics,

And the English are the police.

In Hell...

The Swiss are the lovers,

The English cook the food,

The French run the hotels,

The Italians are the mechanics,

And the Germans are the police.

Cheers,

Steve

P. S. Why the afterlife is so Eurocentric would require a whole other talk show.

163

Day 100
(A Somewhat Anticlimactic)
Milestone
January 28, 2017

Hi All,

Although there is not big news today, the symbolism of reaching day 100 perhaps merits this update. Yesterday's clinic visit was good. Liver function numbers are back to normal, and my white blood cells, neutrophils, hemoglobin, and platelets are all in the normal range as well. Despite those results, I remain immuno-suppressed due to the anti-rejection medication that I continue to take. Next week, they will begin to taper that down, which should ramp up my immunity over the next several months.

Tasha (my favorite clinician) performed my seventh bone marrow biopsy at yesterday's visit to verify that I am cancer-free. I will learn the results at next week's "anniversary" visit with my lead oncologist, but with the numbers cited above, there's reason for optimism. These biopsies involve a needle puncture and aspiration from the iliac crest of the hip bone. I've had them done with just localized lidocaine and no other anesthesia (my choice), so there are brief moments of zinging discomfort and burning. They pass quickly and it's preferable to the lingering effects of a sedative. And, as I told Tasha, if I'm getting stabbed in the back, it's nice that it's someone I've come to trust over multiple clinic visits.

On other fronts, sinus headaches and dry eyes have abated. The rash on my scalp has receded somewhat, although Tasha says it could be an indication of minor graft-vs.-host disease and bears watching. Sue's diagnosis is that since my new immune system (Ralph) is only three months old but will reach maturity within a year or two, this is probably a case of his juvenile acne being played out on my scalp. Since my treatment slightly elevates my risk for skin cancer, I also have an appointment with a dermatologist next week to get a total body skin check and establish a baseline for any future developments.

I had a second appointment with my podiatrist because the previous numbness in my feet has advanced to some tingling and pain across the front of my feet, especially at the end of the day. He suspects I may have two different things going on. First, the already mentioned Morton's Neuroma that predated my treatment but has intensified in recent months. Second, a more generalized inflammation and pain across the front of my feet that may be chemo-therapy-induced neuropathy. Nobody knows for sure, but Tasha agrees this is a possibility. The bad news is that this could continue for months and perhaps longer. Ugh! The good news is that steroid injections above my toes (with a numbing agent because, despite my anesthesia-free bi-opsies, I'm not a masochist about pain) have alleviated much of the discomfort. An upcoming fitting for custom insoles for my shoes should address mechanical issues about how my feet bear my weight.

To sum up, I have dodged all the potentially serious life-threatening complications and side-effects from my cancer, chemo, radiation, and medications to date. I have some relatively minor quality-of-life loose ends that I hope will improve with time and the tapering of medica-tions. As I share my experiences with people of my gen-eration, I am also learning that most of you have some of this stuff (or other such maladies) even without a cancer diagnosis, so it may be, as one of my favorite posters claims, "getting old isn't for sissies."

I'll send an update after next week's clinic visit with biopsy results and an overview of how the next few months should play out. For now, I'll close with the joke.

Joke of the Day:

A guy suffering from amnesia walks into a bar.

After settling in with a drink, he approaches an attractive woman sitting alone and says, "So, do I come here often?"

Cheers,
Steve

As Good as It Gets—with a Footnote
February 2, 2017

Hi All,

This week has been a bit more newsworthy than most. I had my "anniversary clinic visit" today, symbolizing that I'm past day 100 and it's time for some changes. The big headline was my bone marrow biopsy report. They have detected no traces of leukemia in either my bone marrow or peripheral blood. To quote Nelli (my lead oncologist whom I've come to greatly appreciate alongside Tasha), the report is "as good as it gets."

I'm now able to stop one medication and reduce some others. The big change is a gradual 3-month tapering of my anti-rejection medication. I hope this will resolve some lingering side-effects.

This immunosuppression business is quite complicated to a novice like me. When I was just receiving chemo, it was all about the white blood cell and neutrophil numbers. Chemo makes them go down, then your body will recover, and you're good to go. I received more chemo just before my transplant, the numbers went down again, then recovered, but I'm *not* fully good to go.

So, I asked why or how am I still immunosuppressed

with such "good" numbers.

At that point, Nelli went all technical on me, describing all the different components of the immune system and their complex interactions. It turns out this is her area of research, and you know how people can get when you ask them about something that's close to their hearts.

Best I can tell, I have the defenses I need (white blood cells and neutrophils) but the cyclosporine prevents them from firing when needed. It also keeps them from attacking my organs. So, even with good numbers, my immune system remains suppressed as part of the anti-rejection strategy.

There's also the immaturity of my new immune system (Ralph) to consider. As Nelli put it in her charming Armenian/Russian accent, I (or at least Ralph) am like her three-month-old baby, and she feels a bit like a protective mother wanting to minimize my exposure to possible infections. That's why I must wait a full year to restore all the childhood immunizations and vaccinations that were obliterated with my old immune system.

Even with all that, the tapering of the drug means I will gradually be able to resume my normal activities over the next couple of months, although continuing to wear a mask in public places is an advisable precaution. That should be workable at the grocery store or movie theater, a tad awkward in a restaurant, and positively weird should I return to the poker tables at our local casino, but I'm taking it one step at a time.

Meanwhile, in another part of town, I made a return visit to my podiatrist to assess my increasing foot discomfort. He suspects not only the previously diagnosed and localized Morton's neuroma, but a more generalized neuropathy that may be a side-effect of chemotherapy. He sent me on yet another adventure to get some custom insoles.

There, the orthotist brought out what looked like two oversized shoe boxes filled to the brim with foam. I placed my bare feet on the foam and pressed down to create an impression of my feet, which in turn is used to make the insoles. The foam itself was so comforting

I was tempted to wear the shoeboxes right out the door. Along with my N95 respiratory mask and the addition of a clown nose and a fright wig, I could create quite a look, but they insisted on keeping the foam. Insoles to follow next week.

I saw a dermatologist on Monday for a full body skin check because I'm at a slightly elevated risk for skin cancer due to all the medications I've been on. She identified several benign, normal aging things and one abnormality on my upper right arm that concerned her enough to do a biopsy.

Her instincts were on target.

A mere four hours after receiving the good biopsy results about leukemia this morning, I got a call that the skin biopsy revealed a pigmented basal cell carcinoma.

Sounds scary, but it's a localized phenomenon. I'm already scheduled for a thirty-minute excision in a couple of weeks that should resolve the problem. The dermatologist blames a lifetime of sun exposure, but you would think that would be more likely to appear on my left arm—you know, the one we all hang out the car window while driving around because it looks cool. Hopefully that will go smoothly, and I'll add skin checks to my health maintenance routine. In the meantime, I've had enough practice at not freaking out over medical news, so I'll just wait and see what follows.

So, the journey continues. One image that occasionally comes to my mind is of those cats who have had a leg amputated due to an accident or a disease. Works for dogs, too, but I'm more of a cat person. Once healed, does the cat become socially withdrawn, mope in the corner, feel sorry for itself, get depressed, or self-medicate on catnip to the point of addiction?

No, the cat doesn't give it a thought, but rather hops around on three legs, eats voraciously, chases the laser pointer, throws up behind the couch, sharpens its claws on your best leather furniture, sleeps all day, and generally gets on with life. I think cats have something important to teach us.

After all this rather technical talk, perhaps this is a suitable joke.

Joke of the Day:

A brain walks into a bar and orders a pint.

The bartender says, "Sorry, I can't serve you. You're out of your head."

Cheers,
Steve

Tag Team Oncologists and an ER
Adventure
February 13, 2017

Hi All,

Last Thursday I had a "reunion" appointment with Rachel, my first oncologist who oversaw my treatment at Park Nicollet Methodist Hospital from June through September before they shipped me off to the University of Minnesota Medical Center for my transplant. My care is beginning to transition back from Nelli and the U of M staff to Rachel and the Methodist staff. It feels like a symbolically welcome development, not least because it's a much shorter commute when I need to be seen.

Over the next couple of months, I will have blood draws and consultations every two to three weeks, alternating between the two facilities. When I summarized Nelli's recommendations for how to monitor my status as I taper off the anti-rejection drug, Rachel was in complete agreement with the plan. It's nice that the two of them are on the same page.

Once I'm off the anti-rejection drug at the end of April, my care will be almost exclusively with Rachel, with return visits with Nelli every six months or so. I'm not sure who gets the honor of restoring all of my childhood vaccinations, but that'll wait until Ralph (my new immune system) is at least one year old this coming October.

I know there is research out there indicating that female doctors tend to be better listeners, display more empathy, and spend more time with their patients than their male counterparts. I can say without hesitation that my experience with these two doctors has been consistent with these findings. I have come to feel very comfortable with them both and could not have asked for better care.

I was feeling good about all this, and then on Friday I noticed some bilateral swelling in an unusual location on my body. I didn't give it too much thought at the time, but on Saturday morning I googled "lymph nodes" and saw a diagram that indicated that my swelling corresponded precisely with the location of a major group of lymph nodes. I thought about my cancer history, my immunosuppression, some recent weight loss, and some high blood pressure readings, and the totality of those things were enough to scare me right over to the emergency room at Methodist Hospital where they have my voluminous medical history right at their fingertips.

Spoiler alert: this ends well, but it's a good story.

I went through triage quickly, and then after a considerable wait, I was seen by a resident physician. We talked, he examined me, and then he said that he had been a resident there for almost two years and had never seen anything like this. (Uh oh.) He said he would have to consult with a more senior doctor.

After a considerable wait, another doctor arrived, and we began round two of "stump the doctor." We talked, he did an even more thorough examination, and seemed puzzled. He said that given my medical history, we should get a CT scan—incidentally, validating my choice of an ER over urgent care.

After another long wait, they rolled me down to the imaging center, did the scan, and returned me to ER pod #2. After a substantial wait (that's four if you're counting), the senior doctor returned with the results.

The first four words out of his mouth were "Mr. Buechler, I'm sorry…" (UH OH!).

He then clarified that he was sorry they could not offer a conclusive diagnosis (which seemed to bug him), but that the CT scan definitively ruled out any lymph node involvement or abnormality, any cancer, any hernia, or anything else that warranted ongoing concern. He suggested I monitor the condition and mention it at my next scheduled doctor's appointment.

So, after six hours and a $100 co-pay, I left with a final diagnosis of an "abdominal wall bulge." If you think about it, it is less a diagnosis than a description, but so it goes. Given my state of mind when I arrived at the ER, I consider it time and money well spent.

I have to drop by my dermatologist on Wednesday to excise that pesky basal cell carcinoma on my right arm, and then it's full speed ahead.

That's all for now, except for the joke.

Joke of the Day:
A mushroom walks into a bar and orders a drink.
The bartender tells him to get out.
The mushroom says, "Why? I'm a fun-guy."

Cheers,
Steve

Pot Pourri
February 27, 2017

Hi All,

It's been two weeks since my last email and things are still going well, with just a smattering of rather mundane items to report.

The excision of my basal cell carcinoma went smoothly on Wednesday the 15th with the dermatologist. I'm cleaning the wound and changing the bandage daily, and will return to have the sutures removed Wednesday, March 1st.

I purchased some top-shelf New Balance walking shoes—they will never be as white as the day I bought them—and had them fitted with custom-made insoles. Although there is a break-in period, the first impression is good. I hope to be able to walk in them with minimal pain while waiting to see if the symptoms diminish as I taper off my medications and the lingering side-effects of chemotherapy recede.

My blood pressure has been unusually high the last few weeks. The docs think it's the cumulative effect of the anti-rejection medication I'm just beginning to taper down after four months of high doses. We're monitoring and medicating and adjusting doses as needed to get it under control.

I showed my "abdominal wall bulge" to my dermatologist and the physician assistant who saw me for my blood pressure. Neither could identify what it might be ("stump the doctor" score = 4), but neither was concerned about it, especially given the clean CT scan I received in the ER a couple of weeks ago.

Sue and I are trading a common cold back and forth, as we often do in winter. It's oddly reassuring that even with my immunosuppression, it hasn't turned into anything worse.

The most interesting things that happened lately concern how my interactions with my doctors have changed and how that retroactively hints at the risks of the transplant that I seem to have survived quite nicely.

For starters, the physician assistant I met with at Park Nicollet Methodist for my blood pressure commented mid-session that she already knew I was "doing great" because my oncologist had told her that I had been to the U of M for a stem cell transplant and was returning to their care for follow-up treatment.

The last part about "returning to their care" was stated with notable emphasis and enthusiasm, implying that people don't routinely *return* once they are sent off for a transplant. I don't know what happens to them and don't care to think too much about it, but it sounded like it's a pleasantly surprising outcome they don't always see.

There also is a marked change in the tenor of my interactions with both my oncologists and physician assistants. Pre-transplant, they were all professional but clinical, detached, and distant. Post-transplant, they are uniformly personable, chatty, warm, and friendly. I may be reading too much into it, but it feels like they didn't want to invest too much in the doctor-patient relationship until they knew how it would turn out. If so, it underscores the risks I seem to have survived and the degree to which mine is a positive outcome.

On that happy note, here's the joke.

Steve Buechler

Joke of the Day:
A dog walks into a bar and asks the bartender, "Do you have any jobs?"

The bartender says, "Why don't you try the circus?"

The dog replies, "Why would the circus need a bartender?"

Cheers,
Steve

Of Ducks, Lymphocytes, and Anti-rejection Drugs
March 8, 2017

Hi All,

This week we enjoyed watching the ice-out on our little lake (earlier than usual, thanks to the early March temperatures pushing 60 degrees F). This provoked some aerial battles between eagles and crows seeking new food sources, but the pickings were slim. Waterfowl have been scarce during the last two days of 30-50 mph winds, but the geese will soon be patrolling the lake. (What do they call Canadian geese in Canada?) Next week should bring mallards, mergansers, and wood ducks, who are the most entertaining waterfowl we host here on our aptly named Duck Lake.

I'm between medical appointments right now, but I'm still on a learning curve when it comes to my treatment and its rationale. You may recall my being somewhat mystified at why I am still "immunosuppressed" even though my white blood cell and neutrophil counts have been in the normal range for months. A recent visit with a physician assistant provided the clearest explanation yet.

Among the disease-fighting components of the immune

177

system are not just neutrophils (which get all the attention when my "counts" are low) but also lymphocytes. These critters fall into three categories: T cells, B cells and "natural killer" (NK) cells. These guys are the first responders who recognize and attack "non-self" antigens. If these were to be produced by my baby Ralph immune system in sufficient numbers, they would come after my organs and it would not be pretty.

The goal of the immuno-suppressing medication cyclosporine is specifically to reduce my lymphocytes and tell these guys to chill out until they can make nice with my body as their new home. As a byproduct of this process, they are also slow to identify external threats to my body. Hence, I remain "immunosuppressed" or more precisely "lymphocyte-suppressed" (for my own good).

Looking more closely at my blood tests confirms this logic: my lymphocyte counts are at the very bottom of the normal range as an intended effect of the drug.

In this same discussion, my physician assistant referred to the drug as a "really nasty" (if necessary) med. That comment sent me back to rosters of the known side-effects of this widely used anti-rejection medication. Keeping in mind that I have *not* had *most* of the possible side-effects (and *none* of the serious ones), my checklist of symptoms I've experienced is nonetheless impressive. It includes: flushing, hypertension, nausea, altered kidney function, numbness and/or tingling in the feet, weight loss, leg cramps, sinus irritation and congestion, and night sweats. Last, but not least, (given my inconclusive ER visit of a few weeks ago), it turns out that the abdominal swelling that stumped no less than four doctors can also be a side-effect of the anti-rejection med. (Mystery solved? Score one for Web MD and self-diagnosis?)

Thus ends today's bio-chemistry lesson. In practical terms, it means I should continue reasonable precautions about avoiding crowds, wearing my mask when feasible in public, etc. At least now that's easier to do with a clearer understanding of why I'm doing it. The good news is that as I continue to taper off the drug (end date in late April), the lymphocytes should come back up to operative levels but hold their fire against me. For those of you old enough to remember, it's a little like easing up on the clutch while pressing down on the throttle and trying not to stall out the car.

In this age of fake news, alternative facts, and unnamed sources, let me be clear. Today's joke was provided by my good neighbor, Deb, who took a picture of a neighborhood church sign board that displayed this joke. Whether the church got it from a higher authority, I leave to your imagination.

Joke of the Day:
A pervert, a con artist, and a fascist walk into a bar.
The bartender says, "What will it be, Mr. President?"

Cheers,
Steve

One Step Forward, Two Steps Back: Doin' the CMV Shuffle
March 18, 2017

Hi All,

I didn't plan to write so soon, but there's a bit of news to report. Last Thursday, I saw my transplant oncologist (Nelli) for the first time in six weeks. We reviewed my recent symptoms and decided to stop the calcium blocker, which has lowered my blood pressure but caused edema and a rash on my feet. It was a generally good consult. She said that I don't have to wear my mask in public anymore. That opens a world of possibilities for me. It was such an upbeat meeting that she offered two parting handshakes in the last 30 seconds of our little get-together.

The next day, I got a call from a "restricted number." I often trash these because the solicitors and scammers have gotten my cell phone number. This time I answered, and it was Nelli. My immediate thought was that there's no *good* reason to hear from her less than 24 hours after our consultation, and that proved to be the case.

It turns out that overnight testing of my blood draw revealed the return of the cytomegalovirus. For those of you with excellent memories, you may recall that I fought this thing off way back in November and December. It's not uncommon in immunosuppressed folks and it can have some serious complications. However, it also responds well to quick, aggressive treatment.

The sad part is that the virus suppresses the immune system and will depress all the counts that Ralph has so conscientiously maintained for several months now. The sadder part is that the medication *also* suppresses the immune system, so I've got three strikes against my immune system if you count the anti-rejection drug, the virus, and this new medication. If my counts drop too low, they may have to give me transfusions or growth factor injections again, but I'm taking it one thing at a time. Given all that, it probably behooves me to return to my earlier precautions: stay home, limit contact, wear the mask in public, etc.

The treatment is to stop my all-purpose preventive anti-viral drug and substitute the higher strength drug with heavy doses of it for two weeks, then taper it down for six weeks. Before the pharmaceutical insert even gets to doses and cautions, it starts with this warning: "Very bad and sometimes life-threatening blood and bone marrow problems like anemia, low platelet counts, or low white blood cell counts have happened with this drug." To which I say, been there and done that, because this is the same drug that dispatched the virus (but not me) last time and I trust we'll have the same outcome now.

These developments also prompted Nelli to say she wants to see me weekly again. It could be a jealousy thing, because she knows I've been two-timing her with my first oncologist in recent weeks, and you know that romantic saying that you never forget your first oncologist. (Why do relationships always get so complicated?) I'll take her at her word that it's about managing the virus, so we'll do weekly blood draws, testing, and consults until this thing is under control.

Meanwhile, I will exercise my well-honed skill of patience and assume that the big world and all its germs will still be waiting for me when I'm ready to reenter it. Maybe it's good to lay low for a time, given that winter has returned and our little lake has *refrozen*. The waterfowl are scarce after a complete ice-out earlier this month. Even so, the days are getting longer, the sunsets are glorious, and life is good.

Today's closer comes from my buddy, Nik, who (among his many identities) is a marathon runner. That may explain the importance of competitive placement in what follows. So here is your joke.

Joke of the Day:
A man with a toaster walks into a bar. He takes a seat, sets the toaster on the bar, and orders a drink.

The bartender brings his drink and says, "What's up with the toaster?"

The man, who seems rather despondent, says that at the crack of dawn he heard the voice of the Lord, who said, "Come forth and receive the Holy Spirit."

The bartender says, "Wow, so what happened?"

The man says, "I came in fifth and all I got was this lousy toaster."

Cheers,
Steve

A Little News Is Good News
April 3, 2017

Hi All,

There's not a lot to report today, but the news I have is good. I'm aware that my reports are not nearly as dramatic as back in the days of hospitalizations, chemotherapy, radiation, and major side-effects from medications (not to mention downed trees and a damaged roof), but I'll easily trade the drama of then for the tranquility of now.

In the last installment of this melodrama, the anti-rejection drug was raising my blood pressure. It required another medication that brought my blood pressure down but caused swelling and a rash on my feet. We stopped that medication, the swelling and rash abated, and my blood pressure has been behaving itself without medication.

My biggest news is the resolution of the cytomegalovirus. On March 16, it clocked in at 1,097 something-or-other, and I began taking a strong dose of a heavy-duty anti-viral drug. A week later, it was down to 280. As of March 30, the virus was below 137, at which point it was basically undetectable. I'll continue a maintenance dose of the anti-viral drug for several weeks, but it looks like it's resolved. It can always come back because it resides not only in me, but in about 60% of you folks as well.

(Kind of creepy, if you think about it.) With a healthy immune system, you'll never have an outbreak, so remember to thank your white blood cells and neutrophils for their work on your behalf.

I'm feeling good enough to tentatively plan a trip to my office in Mankato this Wednesday, marking my first appearance on campus in a full year. I need to begin tossing files and pruning books, so I can vacate the premises and turn my office over to a new hire by mid-summer. I will also return to campus in late April for some retirement events, and it will take a few visits to completely decamp from my office.

My next medical milestones are the day 180 biopsy (April 14), a consultation to review the results (April 20), and my last dose of cyclosporine (April 27). I've been on that medication since the day before my October 20th transplant, and it deserves serious credit for preventing graft-vs.-host disease. As what one practitioner called a "really nasty drug," however, it also gets the blame for various nagging side-effects that I hope will disappear along with the medication. Not unlike my central line Mr. Hickman, both were good to have and necessary at one point in time, but it's good to put them behind me.

Our last joke ventured onto the treacherous terrain of religion with the guy who came in fifth and only got a toaster; undaunted, today we offer one more religious-themed joke.

Joke of the Day:
A man walks into a bar with a Bible under his arm and orders a soft drink.

The bartender asks how he's doing.

The man says that he keeps trying to hook up with a friend named Matt, but they can never quite connect. He says, "I leave messages for him all over town, and today we almost made the connection."

The bartender asks how he knows that.

The man says, "Well, just beneath my message that said

"John 3:16," he replied, "Matthew 3:20 —just missed you."

Cheers,
Steve

Retinal Recovery and a Spooky Retrospective
April 14, 2017

Hi All,

As you may recall, last August, when I was between chemotherapy treatments and still deciding on my transplant, I had a routine appointment with my optometrist. He saw something troubling and referred me to an ophthalmologist who referred me to a retinal specialist. That diagnosis was bilateral retinopathy with "cotton wool spots" and a retinal hemorrhage in the right eye "likely related to leukemia."

This month I returned to see the ophthalmologist. She drowned my eyes in multi-colored drops and shined an incredibly bright light in my eyes. I couldn't see anything, but more importantly, neither could she.

I heard the welcome words, "no cotton wool spots, no evidence of retinal hemorrhage, the retinopathy is resolved." All credit to the body's natural healing process once we had that pesky leukemia on the run.

I had my 8th biopsy ("celebrating" day 180) today and will get results at a consultation next Thursday. In the meantime, I've been reading Susan Sontag's classic treatise on *Illness as Metaphor* about how diseases like tuberculosis (in the 19th century) and cancer (in the 20th century) have been fraught with or understood through metaphors—cancer as invasive, a war on cancer, a cancer on the body politic, etc.

Midway through her essay, I came upon an arresting footnote. When I underwent "conditioning" the week before my transplant, I received full body radiation and two chemotherapy drugs. The footnote that caught my attention described some harrowing history of one of the drugs I received.

During World War II, an American navy ship carrying a chemical warfare agent was blown up in the Naples harbor. Some sailors died of burns or drowning, but most perished from bone-marrow poisoning and lethally low blood counts. That chemical agent subsequently became a standard treatment for leukemia and part of the conditioning I received before my transplant.

The main difference between me and those World War II sailors is that I was at the University of Minnesota Medical Center awaiting a transplant rather than on a ship in the Naples harbor when I got my dose of that drug. That footnote helped explain to me the 15-20% mortality rate from the transplant itself, because if the new stem cells don't engraft, I'd be left as defenseless as those unfortunate sailors. I suppose the recourse is to identify new genetically-matched umbilical cords and ship them to the hospital while trying to keep the patient alive with no immune system until a second transplant could be performed.

My appreciation of Ralph deepens every day. On a lighter note, here is your joke.

Joke of the Day:
A guy walks into a bar and spots an attractive woman on a bar stool. After gathering his courage, he approaches her and asks, "Can we chat?"

She responds by yelling, "No, I won't come over to your place tonight!"

With everyone in the bar staring, the poor guy creeps

back to his seat, puzzled and humiliated.

A few minutes later, the woman walks over to him and apologizes. "I'm sorry if I embarrassed you," she says, "but I'm a graduate student in psychology. I'm studying human reactions to embarrassing situations."

At the top of his lungs the man responds, "What do you mean, two hundred dollars?"

Cheers,
Steve

Day 180: Taking Off the Training Wheels and Au Revoir?
April 21, 2017

Hi All,

Yesterday was day 180, and my anniversary visit with my transplant oncologist, Nelli. I went there expecting good news, but hearing it in person had quite the impact.

She came into the room and gestured for me to hop on the exam table. While washing her hands with her back to me, she casually remarked "your biopsy was fine."

I reminded her that on day 100 she said the biopsy was "as good as it gets." I asked if we could still use that language, and she enthusiastically agreed.

That conclusion is based on an examination of tissue and fluid from the bone marrow biopsy as well as a peripheral blood sample. Multiple tests found no leukemia anywhere and re-confirmed (through DNA analysis) Ralph's 100% engraftment. Next week I stop the anti-rejection medication (after 188 days) and the vision-blurring, anti-fungal medication I've been taking, but will continue with the anti-viral medication for a full year post-transplant.

Nelli said I don't need to see her until my October anniversary date when Ralph and I can get our childhood immunizations and our one-year biopsy, just to keep tabs on things. I said that after all this time I would miss seeing her.

She reminded me that it's a *good* thing when the patient doesn't have to see their doctor. I will still check in with my first oncologist, Rachel, at Park Nicollet for monthly blood draws to check my immune system, but that's just monitoring.

I can resume any activity I want except getting close to sources of fungal infections, so yard work, gardening, and houseplants are still verboten, but anything else goes. Next month, my health club dues that have been on hold for 9 months will resume. I'll get my money's worth returning to the pool and getting a personal trainer to help me restore the 15-20 pounds of muscle mass I've lost.

It took most of the day to find words that capture my emotional reaction to all this news. At first, I thought I might be delirious from a 15 hour fast required for my early afternoon blood draw. This feeling persisted after eating, and I finally hit upon a phrase that sounds a bit contradictory, but whoever said emotions are logical? I would describe my response as a state of serene euphoria, and I suspect a bunch of natural endorphins are involved. I hope Ralph is in on this too; he deserves it after all he's done for me.

With this welcome news, I anticipated suspending these routine reports. Composing them and receiving your responses has helped keep me sane, but it's time for Ralph and me to take off the training wheels and see if we can stay sane on our own. Having said that, I immediately realized that I benefit so much from the back and forth with you all that I'm not quite ready to halt it altogether.

So, here's my proposal. If there is significant medical news, I'll still report it. If not, I may still send a brief update at longer intervals just to keep in touch. Please know your readership and support have been more valuable than I can easily put into words.

Given this wonderful news, it seems appropriate (in some twisted way) to conclude with what may be the worst joke I have foisted on you in this entire series. The credit/blame goes to my buddy, Nik, for this joke.

Joke of the Day:

A man and a giraffe walk into a bar. They both start drinking heavily.

The giraffe falls off his bar stool and collapses onto the floor.

Shortly after, the man stumbles toward the door to leave.

The bartender says, "Hey, you can't leave that lyin' there."

And the man says, "What do you mean? It's not a lion. It's a giraffe."

Cheers, Adios, Aloha, Au Revoir, Ciao, and Peace,
Steve

6. Coda
(Putting the Pieces Back
Together)

*"Stories have to repair the damage that illness has done
to the ill persons' sense of where they are in life and
where they may be going. Stories are a way of redrawing
maps and finding new destinations."*
—Arthur Frank, from *The Wounded Storyteller*

These final seven reports were sent at monthly intervals from May through October 2017. They report the results of my monthly lab work, provide further reflections on my transition to a new kind of normal life, and describe my growing involvement in various activities as a survivor in the cancer community. The last report provides concluding reflections on my final biopsy and its implications for the way forward.

Dumped by Yet Another Woman (Oncologist)
May 21, 2017

Hi All,

It's been a month since my last email, so I thought I'd report some news and reap my own "writing-as-therapy" benefits.

You may recall that after my 6-month, post-transplant visit on April 20 with my U of M oncologist, Nelli, that she cut me loose. She doesn't want to see me until my one-year anniversary in October. So, I returned to my initial Methodist Hospital oncologist, Rachel, for a good visit last Wednesday where we scheduled monthly lab work.

When I asked if we should also meet monthly, she said she didn't want to see me until August unless the numbers get out of line. That means I've been dumped by two women in the last month, which may be just desserts for my two-timing them with each other.

Before Rachel delivered this news, I asked her to describe my status; am I "in remission," "cured," or what? She said she had no problem calling me "cured," which sounds nice.

Then there is the question of relapse. She said there are no reliable statistics on the probability of relapse for my specific illness/transplant, but that if a relapse were to occur, it's most likely to happen within the first year or two. So rather than waiting for the more conventional five-year window with other cancers, I should know something rather definitive (good or bad) in a shorter time period.

Meanwhile, I'm reading a lot of cancer memoirs. Much of what I'm reading is eerily familiar and oddly comforting; learning how others have been where I've been makes my experience feel less isolated.

But some of what I'm reading is harrowing and humbling. Case in point: David Rieff's grimly titled *Swimming in a Sea of Death* recounts his mother Susan Sontag's death from cancer in 2004 after she survived breast cancer in 1979 and uterine cancer in 1998. He recounts how they were devastated by her 2004 diagnosis of myelodysplastic syndrome or MDS, described by her doctor as a particularly lethal form of blood cancer for which there were no real treatments at the time. The doctor advised waiting tilt it "converted" to full-blown acute myeloid leukemia (AML), which of course, is the disease I was diagnosed with last summer. (Being a high achiever, I skipped right over MDS and went right to AML.)

The only remedy available when Sontag's disease progressed to AML in 2004 was a bone marrow transplant that was contra-indicated for a seventy-one-year-old woman.

Spoiler alert: she had the transplant and perished anyway. In a particularly cruel twist of fate, her MDS/AML was attributed to the chemotherapy drugs used to "successfully" treat her uterine cancer six years before.

To which I say, "Yikes."

Twelve years later when I was diagnosed, the umbilical cord blood transplant I received had become routine at the U of M. They did what they do best, and here I am counting my blessings and feeling like the picture of health, except for my stupid, neuropathic feet, but that's a whole other talk show.

Several of these memoirs also wrestle with finding a "place" in one's life for cancer. While "cure" is the gold standard, the reality of prior illness, the possibility of unpredictable relapse, and the sense of heightened vulnerability will never go away. But beyond that, both I and others I've been reading feel a need to hold on to…what exactly? Not the disease or the side-effects of treatment, but rather the clarifying perceptions that seem inextricably tied to coping with and surviving a life-threatening illness. To put the cancer experience completely behind me—even if I could—risks losing a newfound sensibility that reorders life's priorities. I don't want to lose that. It's an interesting lesson in holding on and letting go. (No, Dr. Freud, we're not talking about your second stage of psycho-sexual development, but thanks for asking.)

Another way of holding on is finding an outlet to share my experience and knowledge with newly diagnosed patients and their caregivers. I'm exploring several options, but my first venture into a transplant support group has been instructive in ways I didn't anticipate. I went to the meeting, assuming I would be the "veteran" at seven-months post-transplant and could be a fount of information for the newbies. Instead, I found myself in a room that included several senior veterans, some newbies, and a few patients who have undergone much more prolonged and arduous treatments than me. While I made a couple suggestions to the newbies, I unexpectedly took away more than I could offer. I was also humbled by the grit and tenacity of my fellow survivors.

Meanwhile, my health club had generously suspended my monthly dues for ten months, but they're charging me for May and it's time to get my money's worth. Tomorrow I meet with a personal trainer to develop a program that will recondition some muscle mass and restore the 15-20 pounds I seem to have misplaced over the last many months. Tuesday, I plan to return to the pool after an 11-month hiatus to see if forty years of lap swimming muscle memory can still get me down and back the length of the pool (and repeat, etc.).

In the category of gallows humor, here's a "bad news, worse news" joke attributed to the poet Joseph Brodsky and recounted in Rieff's book.

A patient comes to see his doctor who says, "I have bad news: you have inoperable cancer and only six weeks to live."

Devastated, the patient blurts out, "What news could possibly be worse than that?"

To which the doctor replies, "We've been trying to contact you for two weeks now!"

Funny, but a bit grim for our taste, so let's conclude with a silly joke compliments (no pun intended—wait for it) of David, a former graduate student.

Joke of the Day:

A man walks into a bar and sits down. He hears a voice say, "Nice shirt."

The man looks around but does not see anyone.

A moment later he hears, "I like your haircut."

Again, he looks around but there is no one there.

The man calls over to the bartender. "Hey, I keep hearing a voice telling me I have a nice shirt and a good haircut, but I don't see anyone. Where is the voice coming from?"

The bartender says, "It's the peanuts. They're complimentary."

Cheers,
Steve

What a Difference a Year Makes
June 17, 2017

Hi All,

This is a good time for an update, for a couple of reasons. For one, it was a year ago this week that I had a biopsy (Monday), received a diagnosis (Wednesday), checked into a hospital (Thursday), and began chemotherapy (Friday). On the one-year anniversary of my hospitalization, I had a much more pleasant day.

It began by reviving a twenty-two-year old tradition with my buddy, John, as we spent the day in a pool hall indulging our mutual passion for the game. We compete, but it's friendly; we don't keep score and we'd rather lose to an excellent shot by our opponent than win with a sloppy shot of our own. Beyond the game, walking into a pool hall has become our way of temporarily leaving the world behind, which may explain our propensity for playing for 6, 8, or 10 hours straight (and once, for 13 hours).

We have a knack for engaging in the kind of silly wordplay that provokes gut-wrenching, tear-inducing, soul-cleansing paroxysms of uncontrollable laughter. This, of course, is not normal pool hall demeanor, and we've had nearby patrons pick up their balls and move to a different table when confronted with our antics. Thursday was that kind of day.

At the 7-hour mark, my neuropathic feet gave out, so we called it a day. I contacted Sue and we headed to a bar poker tournament where she made a deep run before being knocked out of the tournament. I clawed my way through a 45-person field to take second place and a gift certificate for dinner next time. All told, seven hours in the pool hall and four hours at the poker tournament was a much better day than navigating a hospital admission.

On the medical front, I had my monthly blood draw yesterday and my counts and numbers are good so there's no indication of relapse thus far. We'll keep checking them monthly.

I then saw my urologist, who has been monitoring my PSA level (a dubious indicator of possible prostate cancer) since well before my leukemia diagnosis. You don't want this number to go above four, and I had been flirting with numbers in that neighborhood for a couple of years.

When we checked it last fall, it clocked in at 16, but that was a mere three weeks after high dose chemotherapy, which I'm told can wreak havoc with the numbers. We rechecked it this spring and it was down to 8, which is better but still worrisome. My doctor said that if the earlier reading of 16 was in any way indicative of prostate cancer it would not go *down* later, so we're assuming both numbers were artificially elevated by medications and their lingering effects. We'll check it again in six months.

All told, I now have clean bills of health from my ophthalmologist, dermatologist, urologist, and two oncologists. So, you ask, what other issues could there possibly be? Well, just the return of a chronic, low-back issue that recently sent me limping to my chiropractor. It's much better already, but they're recommending multiple treatments and rehabilitation to prevent a recurrence. The financially cool part is that there are two practitioners in the same office with independent insurance authorizations; by seeing both in alternating visits, I can cover up to 18 treatments. So, having been all but abandoned by my female oncologists because I'm doing so well, I now find myself once again seeing two women (chiropractors) at the same time, but they're both cool with it—indeed, they proposed it.

The back issue has temporarily delayed my goal of working with a personal trainer to restore some pounds and muscle mass that I lost during my treatment, but it has not kept me out of the pool. This week, I managed three daily sessions swimming a modest 20 laps each time and gently reawakening those muscles after a year without a workout. It's a far cry from my 50-lap standard from the preceding four decades, but all in good time. It felt wonderful.

Meanwhile, in another part of town, I have now traded a job and salary for retirement and pension. A couple of weeks ago, I fully decamped from my office where I had a few books to deal with. I brought home about 100 titles dearest to my heart, and then let graduate students pillage whatever struck their fancy. The campus library claimed the rest, and they tell me the remnants amounted to 648 books they will either add to their collection or donate to Better World Books.

My retirement transition has been seamless. For forty years as a professional sociologist, I spent three mornings a week closely reading the specialized literature in my field and then doing my own writing, building on that work. I now find myself spending three or four mornings a week closely reading other cancer memoirs. By "reviewing the literature," I hope to make my own memoir a worthy addition to that genre of writing.

In scholarly writing, the goal is to make a new contribution to a field of study; in commercial publishing, it's to compose a profitable commodity to attract a publisher. While the topic and goals are different, my current work routine nonetheless feels eerily familiar and deeply fulfilling. If I'm going to have a retirement crisis, it won't happen until this project is concluded. For the time being, I couldn't be happier practicing my writing craft.

All told, I'm riding a wave of peaceful contentment and appreciation of life that is totally at odds with our insane political reality, and the juxtaposition is quite bizarre.

Next month I will be hosting a "retirement and recovery" party, and all of you are cordially invited to join in

Steve Buechler

the double celebration. For those who can't make it, we'll follow a venerable Italian tradition of pouring extra glasses of wine in your honor.

With thanks to David again, here is the joke.

Joke of the Day:
An empty bottle walks into a bar and orders a drink.
The bartender responds, "I can't serve you; you're already drunk."

Cheers,
Steve

Vivid Imagination, Good Numbers, and Speaking Gigs
July 19, 2017

Hi All,

Well, it's *that* time of the month again. Before I report on my lab work, let's have a little drama.

A couple of weeks ago, I began to notice some atypical fatigue. I was unusually tired throughout the day and exceptionally so by bedtime. I also noticed a bruise on my left forearm—not sure where that came from—my eyes were sore, my pulse was elevated, and I intuitively knew that something was not right.

Fatigue and bruising are classic symptoms of a leukemia relapse. Pair that with a vivid imagination, and my mind went down a rabbit hole to some dark places.

The morning of my lab work, I called in to report my symptoms and to see if they wanted to draw any extra blood to look for possible causes. They added an oncology profile and electrolyte check in addition to the standard hemogram that tracks white blood cells, hemoglobin, and platelets.

That conversation triggered a recollection of two bouts with the cytomegalovirus back in November and again in March. Its leading symptom is fatigue. So, somewhat perversely, I took heart at the possibility that *all* I had was a potentially life-threatening virus (again) rather than a relapse of leukemia. After all, we had tamed the CMV quite effectively with high doses of a targeted antiviral medication, which sounded good given the alternative in my fevered imagination.

I arrived early for my lab work and asked if I could consult with a provider. They paged an on-call nurse who appeared within twenty minutes and gave a persuasive diagnosis based on partial test results and a detailed recitation of my symptoms. To extend the drama a bit further, let's mimic the Sunday New York Times Magazine's periodic column called "Diagnosis." They describe a patient with confounding symptoms and invite readers to guess the cause. In that spirit, now is the time to make your best guess.

The nurse reported that my blood counts were good and unchanged from last month, ruling out any relapse of leukemia. My electrolytes were fine, so we were just waiting on the oncology profile. Meanwhile, she said that based on everything I had reported, she thought I was dehydrated. (Winners claim your prize at window A.)

It clicked immediately. My mainline beverage is coffee all morning, which dehydrates the body and is not counterbalanced by a few gulps of water during the day, much less a glass of wine with dinner (which also has a dehydrating effect). As I was driving home, she called to say the oncology profile was good except for my creatinine level, which measures kidney function. It was slightly elevated—consistent with dehydration and remedied by flushing the kidneys with increased fluids.

Being a good patient, I've been pumping non-caffeinated beverages ever since and my symptoms are improving (stock tip: buy Gatorade). So, thanks to my nurse and kudos to my long-time camping buddy, Becky. For many years as we paddled pristine lakes and hiked hilly portages in the Boundary Waters, her mantra was "Drink more Water!" Becky, you were right then, and you're still right now.

Meanwhile, in another part of town, some unexpected

invitations have dropped in my lap. On the last Saturday of this month, the Blood and Marrow Transplant Unit is having their second annual "Marrow on the Move" fundraiser with a 5K run, walk, and "tot trot" at a local lake. I signed up for the walk (neuropathic feet permitting) and thought about entering Ralph in the tot trot but he's still a toddler, so maybe next year.

I then got a call from my social worker saying they were looking for a transplant survivor to give a talk at the event and she thought I'd be a good speaker. I've accepted the offer and am working on the talk. Since my sense of humor was one of the things that got me through thick and thin, I plan on opening with the lion/giraffe joke and closing with the duck-asking-the-bartender-for-grapes joke. In between the jokes, I'll say serious stuff about being a proactive patient, mindfulness, physical activity, etc., but I can't pass up an audience like that without a couple of jokes.

While a draft of that talk has been simmering on the back burner, I got another call on Sunday morning from the woman who taught the mindfulness class I took before my diagnosis last summer. I had called her recently to thank her for the class and explain how I had utilized her lessons during my treatment. She then asked if I would be willing to give a guest talk at one of her workshops. I agreed, envisioning another community education class of a couple dozen people here in Eden Prairie.

Turns out her call involved a rather different audience. She was about to fly to Connecticut for a two-day conference which was the culmination of a two-year training program for several dozen medical directors and doctors, and the concluding session was on the benefits of mindfulness. She didn't offer me a plane ticket, but rather proposed a teleconference call from my home to their auditorium.

I quickly pulled some ideas together and gave the talk yesterday afternoon. It was a weirdly disembodied experience to speak to a room full of ghost people with no visual cues as to how my message was being received. I laid off the jokes and played it straight, though I did

203

Steve Buechler

get a resounding laugh when I concluded by saying I'd been to enough conferences to know they were in that late afternoon zone where people are stealing glances at their watches and thinking about happy hour.

While I don't want to turn surviving cancer into a career, these speaking opportunities, working on writing, and my monthly transplant support group meetings feel right for now. Indeed, at last night's support group, there was a guy roughly my age who has my diagnosis of AML and is checking into the hospital today for conditioning leading to a double umbilical cord transplant in a week.

It was *déjà vu* hearing him describe it. He voiced some concerns but said he didn't even know what questions to ask. My thought was I can give you answers without you even asking the questions, so I spoke with him after the meeting for about a half hour and left him my phone number if he cares to call me later. It's a good use of my hard-earned experience, and it seems this sort of thing ought to be more institutionalized for the benefit of new patients. Perhaps a new project for me...?

In any event, that's today's news. Without further ado, here's today's joke.

Joke of the Day:
A horse walks into a bar.
The bartender says, "Hey."
The horse says, "You read my mind, buddy."

Cheers,
Steve

Some Writing, Retirement, and Recovery Milestones
August 22, 2017

Hi All,

Well, it's been a busy month here in Lake Wobegon.

I continue working on writing "the thing that might become a book." I hope it will be useful to other cancer patients and those in their social circles.

Meanwhile, on a recent Saturday, Sue and I hosted my retirement (and recovery) party with an afternoon open house. A number of faculty colleagues, graduate students, and the world's best administrative assistant, Karen, and her side-kick and exemplary former student, Jessica (a/k/a Santa Claus from long-ago departmental Christmas parties) made the trip up from Mankato to take part in the festivities.

They were joined by a great group of neighbors and assorted ne'er-do-wells. Some traveled from Milwaukee as representatives of my caregiving Team Wisconsin that saw me through some dark days last winter. Over the weekend, Donna successfully defended her sheepshead crown in two lengthy rounds of card playing.

It was very gratifying, if a bit head-spinning, to see so many different slices of my life come together in one time and place. My only regret was that there wasn't enough time to spend with everyone. Maybe I'll re-retire next year and have another party.

On the following Saturday, I went to "Marrow on the Move," a somewhat creepy title for a genuinely uplifting community building and fund-raising event put on by the Blood and Marrow Transplant Unit that performed my procedure. It was held at a local lake on a picture-perfect day with a short program followed by a 5K run/walk for adults and a "tot trot" for kids.

When I registered, I was issued my purple T-shirt, signifying that I am a patient/survivor along with perhaps 50 other purple shirts in attendance. There were easily 250 red shirts issued to caregivers, family and friends of patients, and another 50 or so gray shirts worn by BMT personnel. In short order, I was able to reconnect with my two social workers, almost a dozen nurses, the dynamic duo of physician assistant Tasha and nurse practitioner Sasha, the doctor who oversaw my actual transplant, and my lead oncologist, Nelli, who has called the shots from beginning to end. I don't know who was left running the shop, but all my principals were in attendance.

I had been nominated by my social worker to give a talk at the event, and after opening remarks by two doctors, it was my turn. I was the only patient/survivor to address the gathering, and my personal story clearly resonated with the crowd and was well-received. It was a challenge to condense it all into 5 minutes, including a bad joke and a well-deserved tribute to the BMT people.

The real high point for me was the walk around the lake. I mingled with various folks along the way, and then Nelli joined me for a one-on-one talk for the final forty minutes of the walk. Given my medical adventures over the last year, it was a powerful experience to be casually strolling around a lake in shorts, T-shirts, and sneakers while amiably chatting with the doctor who oversaw the treatment that saved my life.

The whole day underscored the gravity of what I've been through and my good fortune to still be here. The celebratory reaction that survivors get at events like this is a strong reminder of how profoundly these diseases threatened our lives and how recovery and remission are anything but foregone conclusions.

On the medical front, I'm winding down my chiropractor visits (mission accomplished) and ramping up some acupuncture appointments to see if it can help my feet. As with my oncologists and chiropractors, I'm two-timing a couple of very nice providers who trade me back and forth on office visits. I can't claim any significant improvement, but we'll give it time. A few more sessions should demonstrate if they can reawaken my fried nerves and resolve the numbness and aching that everyone attributes to my pre-transplant conditioning chemotherapy drugs.

This email was triggered by Monday's monthly blood draw/lab work and my meeting with my Park Nicollet oncologist, Rachel. How nice that those numbers, which were once so important (on a daily basis!) have now faded into a monthly footnote. In case you're keeping score, all the numbers on the blood counts and oncology profile were in the normal range, so my borderline platelets from last month have recovered and everything remains good. By the time Rachel stepped into the exam room, I had the numbers from my medical website and commented that they were quite good. She corrected me by saying they were "excellent," so there you have it.

There is one other medical issue to note. A couple weeks ago I had a long-deferred colonoscopy that revealed a benign polyp that will require some minimally invasive surgery to remove. I met with a surgeon today and we scheduled a diagnostic MRI to get more data, to be followed by a consultation with both my oncologists to assess the timing of the procedure vis-a-vis my slowly maturing immune system. We don't want to stress out Ralph after all the fine work he's done. I'll spare you any further details and provide an update when the whole thing is behind me, so to speak.

I ended my marathon visit to Park Nicollet Methodist Hospital by returning to the oncology ward where I visited with two of my "A team" nurses. Jane had nursed me through a 2015 bladder infection as well as my 5 ½ week chemo adventure last summer. Jane has a vivid memory of me from my 2015 stay. On the first night of hospitalization in my life, I woke up groggy and needed to get to the bathroom. I thought it was logical to simply unplug my IV line and go tend to business. Soon, there was blood everywhere. Once she understood the cause, Jane and I had some good laughs (and still do), though the guy who had to clean up after me didn't have much of a sense of humor.

I also reconnected with the world's best nurse, Lynne, who provided superb care (and more than a few laughs) during my "residency" last summer.

As always (and thanks to neighbor, Deb), we close with your joke.

Joke of the Day:
A lawyer, a spy, a mob boss, and a money launderer walk in to a bar.

The bartender says, "You guys must be here to talk about adoption."

Cheers,
Steve

My Victory in a 1K Survivor's Walk
September 19, 2017

Hi All,

Turning up like a bad penny, here is this month's update.

Last month I reported on the 5K run/walk and fundraising event of the Blood and Marrow Transplant Unit where I gave a talk and chatted with Nelli, my transplant oncologist, as we strolled around Lake Nokomis.

This month, the Park Nicollet Frauenshuh Cancer Center held their own fundraising event which I also attended. Last summer/fall, I spent almost 50 nights over three separate Methodist hospital admissions with these folks before going to the BMT unit for my transplant, so I hoped to reconnect with some of the nurses and doctors from those adventures at this fundraiser.

The event at Lake Calhoun/Bde Maka Ska took place on a brisk Saturday morning with a 5K/10K blade, bike, run/walk. It was well-attended, but I had trouble finding any of "my people" among the throngs. As if to prove me wrong, my oncologist, Rachel, then appeared at my side to say hello.

We had a brief chat about the potential of laser treatments for peripheral neuropathy, which she said often provide initial benefits but then require maintenance treatments for ongoing improvement. The down side is that it is considered experimental and would not be paid by insurance. As I was digesting this, she offered a hasty apology and took off to join the 5K runners who had left the starting line.

Much as I enjoy circling lakes with oncologists, my feet were not ready for an actual jog, so I wished her the best and returned to mingling with the crowd.

They then called for the start of the survivor's 1K walk, whose distance and pace were a better fit for my neuropathic feet. At the starting line, I reconnected with my hospital chaplain and a colleague who were waiting to accompany survivors on the walk. The spooky part was that I was the *only* survivor to show up for the walk. No one knew what to make of that, but I sure hope their treatment outcomes are better than just little old me.

So off we went, allowing me to have an extended talk with chaplain Janet. Those of you who know me well may have a hard time envisioning me with a chaplain. When we first met during my initial hospitalization I cautioned her that I was a committed secular humanist and didn't think we had much to discuss. She responded that this was not about what she believed but what *I* believed. That welcoming comment launched a series of memorable conversations about spiritual beliefs, secular morality, meditation practice, emotional rollercoasters, mood swings, identity changes, and much more, spilling across my three hospitalizations.

At this event, all my rigorous training in walking finally paid off as I was the undisputed winner of the 1K survivor event. My chat with Janet continued after our walk, and I also spoke with one of the many doctors who rotated through my hospital care and seemed impressed with my transplant and recovery story. As the event wound down, I returned home with another T-shirt, personalized this time thanks to the spin art folks who let us practice our artistry on their equipment.

I'm continuing with acupuncture for my feet, though it's hard to tell if there is much cumulative progress. I was about to stop after six weeks of treatment when things seemed to improve a bit, but it's clear this is not a quick fix. Laser treatment would be the next step, should I choose to take it.

I'm still a relative newbie in dealing with chronic, nagging health conditions, but I have a newfound empathy for Sue and everyone else who lives with such issues and how damnably hard it is to sort out causes, effects, progress, regress, and helpful remedies or treatments.

The prompt for this report is my monthly lab work which once again came back with everything in the normal range. So far, Ralph is much better than I was last year at maintaining my white blood cells, hemoglobin, platelets, and neutrophils. Speaking of Ralph, his first birthday is approaching on October 20th. I'm getting him a posterior iliac crest bone marrow biopsy and a bunch of baby shots to celebrate the milestone. I'll report back once the results are in. Now, your joke.

Joke of the Day:

A doctor walks into a bar and orders his favorite libation, an almond daiquiri.

That day, Dick the bartender, runs out of almonds and uses hickory nuts instead.

The doctor takes a sip and says, "Is this an almond daiquiri, Dick?"

Dick says, "No, it's a hickory daiquiri, Doc."

Cheers,
Steve

Briefly...
October 20, 2017

Happy First Birthday, Ralph.
Here's wishing us many more!

Ralph's First Birthday: Still "As Good as It Gets"
October 28, 2017

Hi All,

This monthly report brings a few newsy updates and a very positive biopsy result. First, the updates.

On a recent Saturday, I drove to Mankato for our annual department picnic. It was my first such outing as a retired, emeritus professor. I got to meet some promising new faculty members and reconnect with other faculty still serving life sentences. It feels odd not to have an ongoing connection with them, some of whom I've known for decades. For what it's worth, they seem to be doing just fine without me, if you can imagine such a thing.

On the home front, we've made some progress navigating the byzantine labyrinth known as the Minnesota Medical Cannabis Program for Sue. She is now an officially registered patient under the qualifying condition of intractable pain due to psoriatic arthritis and fibromyalgia. I am now an officially registered caregiver for her hav-

213

ing passed my criminal background check. This clears the way for both of us to meet with a state-certified pharmacist who will tailor a dose and form of cannabis presumably suited to Sue's condition. This is all out-of-pocket because insurance won't touch it, but the expense will be worth it if it helps manage her pain better. Now we need to score some pot.

On the medical front, I stopped my acupuncture treatments after some 20 sessions with little relief. I liked both practitioners, but their remedy was not suited to my malady. Future treatment options include laser therapy, boosting B vitamins, or waiting for nerves to regenerate over the next year (they grow really slowly, if at all).

Regarding the cancer community, I have been participating in a workshop through the national Leukemia and Lymphoma Society called Pen my Path, which coaches people to use expressive writing to process the emotional rollercoaster of treatment and recovery from blood cancers. I've shared some of my previous writing and had some online "conversations" with folks who have had similar diagnoses, treatments, or recoveries. We are a very diverse group in terms of geography, age, gender, and just about every other social status, but sharing a life-threatening illness has a way of revealing a common humanity beneath the diversity.

I recently attended the "Light the Night" ceremony sponsored by the Leukemia and Lymphoma Society of Minnesota. More than 3,000 people participated in a walk across the Stone Arch Bridge in downtown Minneapolis just after dusk. Our lanterns—red for supporters, white for survivors, and gold to commemorate those who have died—did indeed light up the night, along with a laser light show bouncing off high-rise buildings on either side of the Mississippi River. It was sobering to see the survivors as the smallest of the three groups, but at least there were more of us than at the survivor walk where I was the only participant.

At Light the Night, multiple speakers paid tribute to those who had passed away, but the stories seemed skewed toward those with my disease of AML, which one speaker characterized as "the deadliest of the blood cancers." I'd never heard it put quite that starkly and don't know if it's technically accurate, but it *was* a tad unnerving. Fortunately, I know a non-random sample when I see one. Nonetheless, my plan is to continue to survive this disease and help balance out the statistics.

On a more positive note, Ralph and I had our anniversary biopsy on his October 20th birthday. Afterwards, I strolled over from the clinic to the hospital where Ralph first came on board during my transplant. While roaming the halls, I reconnected with several of my nurses who gathered round to hear my tale of survival. They clearly welcomed the interruption in their daily routines and thanked me for stopping by. One nurse commented "we never get to see the ones who make it out of here." Her tone suggested my positive outcome was not necessarily the norm, providing another reminder of how precarious my situation was until Ralph saved the day.

That set the stage for my anniversary visit this past Thursday with my transplant oncologist, Nelli, to get my biopsy results. This was my first biopsy since the 6-month mark in April, and because this is a cancer that can return in sneaky and subtle ways, I confess to having more than a little anxiety while awaiting the results.

I was preparing myself for a fateful encounter when someone came in with a mundane survey as part of a research study. There were many questions about my physical health and emotional state, and I jokingly reserved the right to change my answers once I had the biopsy results.

Then another nurse came in with various vaccinations and immunizations for Ralph; they explained that he could tolerate the dead viruses now, but the live vaccines must wait until year two when he is fully operational. I took this as a good sign because it would be downright goofy to immunize and vaccinate a patient who had relapsed into leukemia and would require new rounds of chemotherapy that could compromise those protections.

When Nelli finally arrived, she set some papers on the desk, asked me to sit on the examining table, and asked how I was.

I said she knew the answer better than I did, pointed to the paperwork, and asked about the biopsy results. She said it was all fine, and we proceeded to review the bone marrow tissue and fluid analysis, peripheral blood results, and genetic findings. She summarized by saying it was still "as good as it gets." Bottom line, there is no evidence of any leukemia or other abnormalities by any of these measures, and the genetic data reconfirmed Ralph's 100% engraftment. I think we're talking long-term relationship here.

As we reviewed my year of clean biopsies and no graft-vs.-host disease, she called me an "outlier" who had the best possible outcomes at every critical juncture of treatment. A relapse is still possible, but that is most likely within the first eight months and I'm past that benchmark. Having dodged multiple perils over the last year, my five-year survival rate has improved from about 50% at transplant to upwards of 80% going forward. I'm not out of the woods, but I'm at the edge of the forest. Given all the recent reminders of how deadly my disease can be, I'm feeling humbled, mystified, and grateful for my good fortune.

Reaching the one-year mark in good shape means I can stop my last two post-transplant medications and retire my mammoth pillbox. It also means there are no longer any restrictions on my activity due to suppressed immunity. With impeccable timing, the neighbor who has been mowing our lawn all summer came by Thursday morning to vacuum up all the leaves and put the yard to rest for the season.

Two hours later, Nelli cleared me to do yard work but alas, there's nothing left to do till next year. I think I played that one just about right, eh?

Final evidence of my good fortune came in a phone call from my dermatologist's office. I've been seeing her every six months because immunosuppression can increase the risk of skin cancer. She had previously detected and excised a small basal cell carcinoma last spring. My fall skin check had detected another suspicious spot on my scalp which they biopsied, but the results came back negative with no evidence of skin cancer. So, my record on biopsies this week has been excellent.

Last April, I pondered ending these reports. Now seems like another natural end point, but my past behavior suggests I won't resist the occasional update. Whether I do or not, please don't hesitate to check in with me. Let me offer one more thanks for being such good correspondents throughout this odyssey. The support that all of you have offered means more than I can say, and I will never forget it.

As time goes by, we close with this joke.

Joke of the Day:
The past, present, and future all walk into a bar. It was tense.

Cheers,
Steve

Epilogue: Fashioning New Identities

"For wounded storytellers, the return from illness brings the responsibility to teach others so that not only sick people can 'know what health is.'"
—Arthur Frank, from *The Wounded Storyteller*

My odyssey is a story of diagnosis and treatment, recovery and survival, lessons and transformations, and multiple identity changes. At the cellular level, I am a new person given my merger with Ralph whose DNA and blood type have become my own. On existential and social levels, I have transitioned from being a seemingly healthy person to a cancer survivor and from being an employed professor to a retired sociologist (with the honorary title of professor emeritus, which lets me park in the campus pay lot for free).

My fusion with Ralph is the most distinctive, biological

aspect of my story, so I begin with a succinct summary of how we learned to get along. I then offer some final reflections on identity transformations and my new membership in the remission society of wounded storytellers.

On Recovering from a Stem Cell Transplant

On the first day that I was hospitalized, one doctor outlined short-term and long-term treatment options. The latter included a stem cell transplant, which he delicately referred to as "not for the faint of heart." As I learned more about it, I came to appreciate his comment but nevertheless concluded that a transplant was my best (or least bad) option for long-term treatment.

I was subsequently advised that if I survived the transplant, I would face a prolonged recovery period marked by several benchmarks. The first was being discharged from the hospital. I was told to expect a three- to five-week hospital stay after my transplant.

Much to my surprise, my doctors actually considered discharging me a mere one and a half weeks after the procedure, but an infection kept me in the hospital for another week. Even so, my discharge two and a half weeks after my transplant was on the early end of what I had been told to expect. My most significant recovery benchmark immediately followed. A biopsy performed three weeks after the transplant revealed that Ralph's stem cells were 99% engrafted and no residual leukemia was found.

The next benchmark was my first month at home when my caregivers were essential. They drove me to daily clinic visits for blood draws and provider consultations. During the first week, I received daily transfusions of platelets and one transfusion of red blood cells. Several more transfusions as well as injections of growth factor medications to spur new white blood cells followed over the next couple weeks. By the middle of the third week, they gave me a few days off from daily clinic visits.

That first month was when I felt the side-effects from my treatment most keenly. The lingering impacts of chemotherapy and radiation, the engraftment process, and the multiple medications combined to produce several memorable symptoms. There were aches and pains from the engraftment itself, and ongoing bouts of nausea as a delayed reaction to the chemotherapy and radiation I had completed over a month before.

But mostly, there were staggering levels of fatigue as my body underwent this transformation and Ralph commenced to build me a new immune system. I was sleeping eight to nine hours a night but still required lengthy naps in the late morning and late afternoon. I couldn't stay awake for more than four hours at a time and was totally exhausted by nightfall. I felt like a rag doll as I dragged myself through this period. Given that I was an adult with a baby's immune system, however, I reasoned that my nights were for me and the naps were for Ralph.

After this intense month, my symptoms gradually abated, and my energy and activity slowly increased. The next important benchmark was "day 100" when another biopsy re-confirmed Ralph's full engraftment and no residual disease. This was also the date I began tapering my anti-rejection medication. I followed my pharmacist's guidelines and very gradually decreased this medication over a three-month period. The prolonged tapering was designed to gently bring Ralph up to speed while avoiding any internal warfare between my old body and his new immune system.

I had been told there was a 60-70% chance of acute (within the first 100 days) graft-vs.-host disease in cases like mine, but I had no symptoms that could be attributed to this cause. That happy result reduced my chances of chronic (after the first 100 days) GVHD to 20%. Although it can appear up to two years after transplant, I've had no symptoms as of this writing. It would appear that Ralph and I have made peace with each other.

The next benchmark was day 180 (six months after transplant) when my eighth bone marrow biopsy again confirmed full engraftment and no residual leukemia. My final benchmark was my year one biopsy which reconfirmed full engraftment and no residual leukemia. I was then able to stop my remaining transplant-related medications, resume all my normal activities, and restore some of my childhood vaccinations. Biopsies will still recur every two years, while lab work every other month will provide an early warning system of any recurrence of the disease.

My decision to have the transplant was a good one. As in poker, however, it's easy to applaud your decisions when you win the pot. In my case, I feel as if I've won the jackpot. I started with what felt like no good options, selected the least bad one, travelled a long, convoluted path, and reaped a happy outcome. If my story helps anyone else navigate the process and weather the treatment, then one of my goals in writing this book will have been served.

On Self Transformations

While it feels as if I have *returned* to my life, this obscures the fact that this odyssey *was* my life and not a hiatus from it. As I have re-engaged with the many activities I put on hold, I've done so with a new appreciation for things I used to take for granted, a deeper empathy for other people's struggles, and a profound sense of gratitude at being in the world. Although I do not subscribe to the "cancer will make you a better person" school of thought, it's hard to deny the altered perceptions arising from this experience. Along with the practice of mindfulness, it has given me a new set of lenses through which to see the world and has changed me in ways I can't yet fully articulate.

This identity transformation overlapped with another as I went from employed professor to retired sociologist. I had planned a final year of teaching with plenty of time to weed out four decades of accumulated books, journals, files, student projects, and all the other office paraphernalia one acquires over the years. Instead, I spent my last academic year on sick leave, so disengaging from my professional role was compressed into half a dozen campus

Steve Buechler

visits in the spring of 2017.

On those occasions, I gleefully dispatched thousands of department, college, and university documents that I never bothered to prune as they became outdated. But the books were another matter. I began acquiring academic books as an undergraduate in 1969 and never stopped. To share an academic's secret, I hadn't consulted the great majority of those books in many years. But, to use a famous sociologist's phrase, they made for a very impressive "presentation of self" when students came to my office.

At a deeper level, however, these books were artifacts of my core identity and lengthy career as a professional sociologist. As noted in one of my last reports, I had to dispense with the vast majority of those books, retaining only about 100 favorite titles as a symbolic link to my professorial identity. It was a poignant lesson in letting go.

While I will always retain my identity as a sociologist, I don't anticipate doing any more scholarly publishing. The academic game of reading, quoting, and citing everyone else doing similar work before you can make your case is too time-consuming, and life is too short. I will always enjoy writing, however, and my work on this book has thereby served multiple purposes.

First, the original reports were simply to convey my medical status and reflections to family, friends, colleagues, and neighbors. Second, and more profoundly, this writing-for-others quickly became therapy-for-me by bringing narrative coherence to chaotic experiences. Third, refashioning these reports into a book reaffirmed my writerly identity even as I left academic publishing behind. This work has been an antidote to whatever psychic wounds might otherwise have accompanied retirement.

Like my transition into retirement, incorporating cancer into my identity remains a work in progress. As I read other cancer memoirs to identify the potential market for mine, I found myself still processing my odyssey through their stories. As noted in one of my last reports, it has been eerily familiar and oddly comforting to find similar descriptions of chemotherapy effects, nausea treatments, immunosuppression risks, diagnostic scans, nursing styles, and physician idiosyncrasies. To offer one more trivial but striking example of the latter, I'm betting other patients can confirm my observation that hospital doctors are perhaps the only visitors who never return the folding chair to its former location after a bedside chat. ("It's because doctors *never* clean up after themselves," according to a social worker who'd best remain anonymous.)

The similarities in these accounts by fellow travelers reduces my sense of isolation and makes me feel part of a larger community. Much the same can be said of the transplant support groups I've joined, the fundraising events I've attended, and the talks I've given. Beneath a dizzying diversity of diagnoses, treatments, and prognoses, we share a common humanity as we collectively fashion new identities as cancer patients and survivors.

On Becoming a Wounded Storyteller

As I was completing this project, a colleague suggested that I read Arthur Frank's book on *The Wounded Storyteller.* Frank's work retrospectively overlaid a whole new level of insight into my own narrative, its connections to others' stories, and how patients struggle to retain their personhood in the face of a life-threatening illness and technically-driven treatment.

The author suggests that storytelling by ill persons can play a crucial role in shifting them from a passive to a more active role in their illness. While doctors may insure the patient's survival, telling their story can maintain the person's integrity. Put differently, while people may have to surrender their bodies to medicine, they may retain their core self by telling their story.

It was not always so. In premodern times, illness was attributed to unknowable and uncontrollable external forces, and it was fatalistically accepted.

In modern times, illness became colonized by technical expertise as the physician speaks for the disease. In our emerging postmodern era, however, people's stories about their illness gain primary importance. Such stories can create what Frank calls the "remission society" of people who have been ill, are now better, but could become ill again. These people are on a "permanent visa status" between feeling well and being sick. Storytelling rescues them from the medical colonization that would otherwise reduce them to being passive patients in an asymmetrical power relationship.

The importance of storytelling emerges when illness creates what the author calls narrative wreckage. Temporality is shattered when illness fractures the links between a known past, a comprehendible present, and an expected future. The onset of illness can rupture a formerly sensible life, and it begets further ruptures in one's daily routines (as any hospital patient can attest) as medical case notes threaten to displace a coherent self. By telling our stories, these ruptures can be repaired as ill persons reclaim their identity.

Frank describes three types of stories that may emerge out of illness. Restitution narratives take the form of "I was healthy, then I was sick, now I am (becoming) healthy again." In such accounts, the patient's body is analogous to a broken-down car, the physician is an able mechanic, and the patient is a passive bystander drinking bad coffee in the shop's waiting room. Patients hope to get better and tell their own restitution stories, but they remain ones in which a physician's active intervention restores the sick body of a passive self that is sidelined by technical treatments. These restitution stories are the medically and culturally approved way we think about illness: when something is broken, we get it fixed and move *on.* Nonetheless, it leaves something important out of the picture as the person is reduced to a body needing repairs and the self is sidelined by the doctor's expertise.

The coherence of restitution stories is lacking in what Frank calls chaos stories. Without having a narrative order, coherent sequence, or discernible causality, these stories carry no expectation of recovery or illusion of control. These stories are threatening to the patient, but also to physicians because the stories are an unspoken critique of their inability to fix things.

By their very nature, chaos stories cannot be told as much as they are experienced by ill persons as being overwhelming. They can overtake any sense of a coherent self and an orderly world for a patient. Despite the ill person's sense of helplessness and the physician's dislike for such stories, these stories must be recognized before the patient can reclaim their personhood.

Quest stories are explained as Frank's third type, and the only one in which the teller assumes center stage. In these stories, the patient accepts their illness and seeks to use it, believing that something is to be gained by their experience. Reflecting my choice of the word odyssey, such stories can involve a recursive experience: the patient takes a trip in order to discover what kind of trip it is, and then finds meaning that can be passed on to others.

There is heroism in quest stories, but it isn't the physician vanquishing the disease but rather the stoic patient persevering through suffering. As these patients become wounded storytellers, they derive new meaning in their life from re-telling their illness.

By fashioning quest stories, these people become not just survivors but witnesses with a responsibility to share their stories. Such stories may include the insights that life is really worth living (in ways that only ill persons may fully appreciate), that suffering is an intractable part of the human condition, and that there is a mutuality of need linking ill persons and their caregivers.

Whereas restitution stories offer a specific hope of getting better, quest stories nourish an "intransitive hope" that accepts an open-ended future. This mind-set fosters a quiet courage in a recovering patient to find virtue and pursue excellence in whatever circumstances may unfold in an unknowable future.

As I digested Frank's ideas, I realized I have become a wounded storyteller. Along the way, all three types of storytelling had appeared in my own accounts.

My odyssey began as a chaos story. Upon my hospital admission, I had no clear understanding or sense of control over what was happening to me or to Sue. It seemed like anything could (and did) happen. My fractured impressions nicely fit Frank's description of chaos stories as proceeding through multiple, destabilizing events linked only by the phrase "and then" repeated over and over.

Two weeks after my hospitalization, I had written my first reports and my story took a turn. By then, I had learned more about my disease, the short-term treatment I was receiving, and the long-term options for further treatment. In effect, my doctors were telling me a restitution story about how I had been healthy, then I became sick, and here is how we plan to make you better.

While my medical personnel and treatment provided the data for my restitution story, I played an active role by narrating it through my ongoing reports. In order to convey my experience to others, I had to comprehend it myself. My "audience" became the prod for my own self-understanding, as writing-for-others seamlessly became therapy-for-me and a means of maintaining a coherent self.

The next turn in my narrative occurred after my day 180 consultation. I was six months out from my transplant and had tapered off my anti-rejection medication and its unwelcome side-effects. That turning point sparked a qualitative shift in my mindset. For the first time, I was able to accept that I had weathered my treatments, that they had been successful, and that I was actually better. I then described my mood as serene euphoria, but it came with a powerful urge to reach out and share my story.

With Frank's insights, I can now reinterpret this period of my life as the beginning of a quest story. As I have reached out through support groups, peer counseling, speaking engagements, writing workshops, fund-raising events, and a survivorship conference, I have met the responsibility to share my story. In each case, I responded not to an external obligation, but rather an internal motivation to forge new connections with other members of the cancer community.

My peer counseling with current transplant and blood cancer patients has suggested a corollary to the idea that survivors have a responsibility to tell our stories. I now believe that we also have a responsibility to be witnesses to the stories of other cancer patients. Doing so widens the circle and broadens the community of people who may become authors of their own lives and fashion their own quest stories.

Hearing others' stories has also enriched my understanding of my own odyssey. It has tempered that part of me that wants to believe I have reached a definitive conclusion in a restitution story and that I am forever cured of this disease. It reminds me that I can never know that with certainty. So, as a good citizen in the remission society, I must remain cognizant of the insights afforded to me by quest stories. Rather than a specific hope for permanent recovery, I have an intransitive hope that accepts an open-ended future, and I seek to live well in whatever circumstances may unfold. It seems the wiser course.

While I didn't have the language of "intransitive hope" at the time, the idea was already part of me when I attended a university luncheon for retirees shortly after my day-180 milestone. When pressed on the question, I responded that my retirement plan is to mindfully embrace and mindlessly revel in the sweetness of life. The rest will take care of itself.

Acknowledgements

Many wonderful people supported me throughout my odyssey, and my deep gratitude goes out to all of them. First and foremost, I am grateful to the anonymous parents who donated their newborn children's umbilical cords to a donor bank so that someone like me would have a chance for a longer life.

At Methodist Hospital, Dr. Rachel Lerner oversaw my initial treatment, assisted by Mary Spengler on daily hospital rounds. My "A team" of nurses included Lynne Senftner, Deb Fischer, Val Schwantes, and Jane Kamau Scott, along with the ever-upbeat nursing assistant Van Tran. Kudos also to nurse manager and all-around problem-solver Andrea O'Hern. Finally, my thanks to Janet Stark, who shattered all my stereotypes about hospital chaplains.

At the University of Minnesota Medical Center, Dr. Nelli Bejanyan oversaw my subsequent treatment with the assistance of Dr. Shernan Holtan and Sasha M. Skendzel. My most excellent transplant team consisted of Dr. Holtan, Dr. Liz Levin, my lead nurse Cassi Johnson, and

Roya Connocholia. Throughout my stay, Nicole Ullman was an exemplary social worker providing relevant advice and logistical support. After leaving the hospital, Tasha Kell provided excellent care on subsequent clinic visits.

My spouse Sue Scott has supported me throughout our partnership and provided an indelible model of perseverance and resilience in the face of her own medical challenges. During my first month post-transplant, my "Team Wisconsin" consisting of Jerome Buechler, Dave Schroeder, and Donna Skenadore provided round-the-clock care and friendly competition at the card table. My long-time colleague and friend Tom Schmid played utility infielder by plugging the gaps in Team Wisconsin's game plan and keeping me supplied with good books and scintillating conversation. My sister-in-law Jan Mansell provided unfailingly cheerful house-sitting and taxi service on short notice for both Sue and me when we needed it most. Thanks also to Mike Whaylen for multiple hospital transports.

Our neighbors Doug and Deb Marston, Colleen and Mike Zenk, Pat Duryee and Jerry Cronoble, Judith and Guy Thompson, Vicki and Tom Lindquist, and Joyce and Dan Waverly helped us out in myriad ways over many months and provided an exemplary model of community support. I was also sustained by all my email correspondents, many of whom routinely provided good advice, supportive comments, thoughts and prayers, and a backlog of bad jokes to accompany my email missives.

When I sought a larger audience for my story, Brittiany Koren at Written Dreams Publishing was immediately and enthusiastically supportive of this project. We "clicked" during some initial phone calls, leading to a smooth, professional collaboration that brought this book to fruition, and I am very grateful for her support.

If you enjoyed *How Steve Became Ralph*, you may enjoy reading other memoirs published by Written Dreams Publishing. Check out our website at: writtendreams.com.

Lame Brain

Rick Roberts

Approximately 1.7 million people experience a TBI in the United States every year, with accidental falls being the leading cause. A multiplatinum rock star's life meets an unexpected detour when a bump on the head reveals itself to be a Traumatic Brain Injury (TBI). Told with honesty and humor, *Lame Brain: My Journey Back to Real Life* is Rick Roberts' story of his entangled afflictions of TBI and Alcoholism. Rick openly shares the story of how he confronted these challenges. True to his talent for writing award-winning lyrics and melodies, Rick gives the world a story of healing told in his own compelling voice. He details the routines he created to reclaim his mobility, coordination, and sobriety.

About the Author

Steve Buechler is a native of Milwaukee, Wisconsin, where he attended UW-Milwaukee and financed his undergraduate education by playing the drums in a rock and roll band. After earning a couple more academic degrees, he had a thirty-one-year career at Minnesota State University, Mankato, where he taught sociology and published on social movements and critical sociology.

His favorite pastimes include paddling Minnesota's Boundary Waters Canoe Area Wilderness, cruising the Mediterranean, playing poker in Las Vegas, and patronizing a local pool hall. He lives in Eden Prairie, Minnesota with his wife Susan Scott.

One year before his retirement date, he was diagnosed with acute myeloid leukemia and treated with chemotherapy, radiation, and a double umbilical cord blood transplant. Throughout this time, he turned his writing skills to narrating his cancer odyssey. While doctors treated his disease, telling his story maintained his sanity. His academic website is http://sbs.mnsu.edu/soccorr/faculty/buechler or you can find him on Facebook @SteveBuechlerAuthor.

CPSIA information can be obtained
at www.ICGtesting.com
Printed in the USA
LVHW032300090320
649432LV00005B/488

9 781733 503426